HISTORY'S ANTHROPOLOGY:
THE DEATH OF WILLIAM GOOCH

Association for Social Anthropology in Oceania

ASAO Special Publications:

Ivan Brady, Series Editor
Deborah Gewertz, Associate Series Editor

No. 1 Marshall Sahlins, *Historical Metaphors and Mythical Realities: Structure in the Early History of the Sandwich Islands Kingdom.* Ann Arbor: The University of Michigan Press, 1981.

No. 2 Greg Dening, *History's Anthropology: The Death of William Gooch.* Washington, D.C.: University Press of America, 1988.

ASAO Special Publications No. 2

HISTORY'S ANTHROPOLOGY:
THE DEATH OF WILLIAM GOOCH

To James Boon .

[handwritten inscription] Still thanks for many inspirations

Greg Dening [signature]

Greg Dening

UNIVERSITY
PRESS OF
AMERICA

ASAO

Lanham • New York • London

Co-Published by arrangement with the
Association for Social Anthropology in Oceania

Library of Congress Cataloging-in-Publication Data

Dening, Greg.
History's anthropology : the death of William Gooch / Greg Dening.
p. cm.—(ASAO special publictions ; no. 2)
1. Gooch, William, 1770 or 1–1792—Death and burial. 2. Hawaii—
Discovery and exploration. 3. Hawaii—Historiography.
4. Explorers—Hawaii—Biography. I. Title II. Series.
DU627.D46   1988
996.9'02—dc 19   88–14860 CIP
ISBN 0–8191–7032–1 (alk. paper)
ISBN 0–8191–7033–X (pbk. : alk. paper)

Typeset by Virginia L. Freeman MacOwan, Waterloo, Canada

All University Press of America books are produced on acid-free paper.
The paper used in this publication meets the minimum requirements of
American National Standard for Information Sciences—Permanence of Paper
for Printed Library Materials, ANSI Z39.48–1984.

For

The Association for Social Anthropology in Oceania

A Gift to their Fellowship

For

Marshall Sahlins

A Gift for Many Gifts

CONTENTS

ILLUSTRATIONS

EDITOR'S PREFACE

William Gooch, astronomer aboard the supply ship *Daedalus*, and two of his cohorts were murdered behind the beach at Waimea on the Hawaiian island of Oahu in 1792. "By any measure of events that change the course of human development or exemplify great movement in human thought," Greg Dening says, the death of the twenty-one-year-old Gooch "was and is of no great importance." The event gained special notice in Gooch's immediate family, for obvious reasons, and to some degree in the wider world because Gooch was a Cambridge man and because his commander, Lt. Richard Hergest, was one of the other victims. But the fate of all three men was just as easily swept from view as part of that expansive wave of Strangers who came to the Pacific from elsewhere "for reasons of discovery or empire or trade or religion." The resurrection of Gooch's story, partial and interested though it must be, is thus owed almost completely to Dening's masterful pursuit of the pieces. Gooch's family would be grateful for the effort, and the young man himself undoubtedly would be flattered by it. For us there is a broader point: proceeding with the utmost in empathetic *génie*, Dening moves the search for Gooch and his times through the catacombs of inaccessible archives and the rocky waters of interdisciplinary research and ends up in intellectual territory that historians and anthropologists everywhere will appreciate.

The whole affair of Gooch's death "made History in the ways History is always made, by the selective transformations of events and experiences into public cultural forms of narratives." Wary of those who claim to understand this texted "double helix of now and then," however, Dening knows that events can be possessed in their meanings in culturally-different ways, like so much "Cargo," as they cross the beaches that separate cultures and individuals. The Hawaiians may have killed Gooch because (like sharks, gods, strangers, and chiefs) he had "sparkling eyes." Dening asks where *that* fits into our understanding of Gooch's death and he explores what it might show us about the ways history can be both metaphor of the past and metonym of the present. By tracking the elusive evidence of Gooch's life from Cambridge to Waimea and nesting it in the rich symbolic and cultural circumstances of his death, Dening enjoins the story of "two of humanity's main preoccupations–the Past and the Other"–and he gives us the foundation for history's anthropology. The archaeology of knowledge has no better ground; with Dening as *directeur*, the quest is brilliant.

Ivan Brady

Department of Anthropology
State University of New York College, Oswego
March 1988

ACKNOWLEDGEMENTS

Ivan Brady first introduced me to the fellowship of the Association for Social Anthropology in Oceania. He believed I might have a sentence to add to the discourse begun by Marshall Sahlins in *Historical Metaphors and Mythical Realities*. When illness and my changing perspectives delayed my manuscript, Ivan was always supportive and inspirational. He is bolder than I. He knows not only that anthropology has a poetic. It can also be a poem. Marshall Sahlins and I shared days and classes at the University of Hawaii and the University of Chicago. I was embarrassed that I, being so old in the trade, needed to learn so much. He being the scholar he is, will see how much I still have to learn. Around me all the time I have my wife Donna's loving care, and friends like Inga Clendinnen, Rhys Isaac and Kenneth Lockridge to tease my gnomic tendencies.

My pilgrimages in pursuit of William Gooch led me around the world and left me in debt in every place. Dr. John Pickles, historian of Cambridge University, and poet too, made paths for me through University thickets. Cynthia Timberlake of the Bishop Museum's Library responded generously to any request I made. Indeed the list of institutions and places where archivists and librarians gave me gracious help is long: Gonville and Caius Archives and Library, Norwich Public Records Office, the National Maritime Museum (Greenwich), Mitchell Library (Sydney), Alexander Turnbull Library (Wellington), Baker and Tozzer Libraries (Harvard). Cambridge University Library has permitted me to use and quote William Gooch's papers and to publish his drawing of the *Daedalus*. The Bishop Museum, Honolulu, has permitted me to reproduce William Ellis's painting of Waimea.

My University, Faculty of Arts and Department of History have always supported my research and writing with leave and grants. Lynne Wrout cheerfully and generously added to her many burdens in administering the Department of History in overseeing the preparation of the typescript. She knows my chairman's dependence on her, and my gratitude. Pat Biciacci and Margaret Anderson were infinitely patient with me in typing and re-typing my thoughts and after-thoughts and after-after-thoughts.

Greg Dening

Department of History
University of Melbourne
September 1987

FIGURE 1: WILLIAM GOOCH'S DRAWING OF THE *DAEDALUS*.

PROLOGUE

"WE THOUGHT THEY WERE GODS BECAUSE OF THEIR SPARKLING EYES"

William Gooch died behind the beach at Waimea on the island of Oahu in the Hawaiian chain on 12 May 1792. Hawaiian *pahupu* ('cut-in-two') killed him there with Lieutenant Richard Hergest, commander of the supply ship *Daedalus,* and Manuel, a Portuguese sailor. Gooch, the astronomer, and Hergest, the naval agent commanding the hired merchant vessel, were on their way to join Captain George Vancouver's expedition to the northwest coast of America. They had expected to rendezvous with Vancouver at Kealakekua Bay on the island of Hawaii, but they had experienced a delayed and slow voyage and had missed Vancouver before he returned to Nootka Sound. They had gone on to Waimea to water their vessel.

Thirteen years before, Hergest had made that short trip from Kealakekua to Waimea. He had been a midshipman on the *Resolution* on Captain James Cook's third voyage of discovery. Cook had been killed at Kealakekua. An irresolute *Resolution,* shaken by the killing of its captain, had sailed to Waimea. The ship had passed along the northern shore of Oahu, on the windward side, and discovered the island's fluted palisade of cliffs behind lush, green lowlands. The whole shore was rich with crops and people. At Waimea these explorers found a river flowing out of a forked valley. The water was brackish where the river reached the sea, but it was sweet and deep behind the sandbar. The *Resolution* had a troupe of young girls aboard. The girls had serviced the crew at Kealakekua even in the bloody days of the *Resolution's* revenge for Cook. At Waimea the girls danced for them a *hula* they had not seen before. It was something of a hornpipe, the sailors said, but lascivious in the extreme. Then the girls told the people of Waimea the extraordinary story of Lono's death at Kealakekua, at which there was such a buzz that the *Resolution's* officers thought better of taking the girls further and left them at Waimea. Waimea was the bay Hergest remembered in 1792 when he wanted water for the *Daedalus.*

The *Daedalus* stood three miles off shore, anchored on a foul bottom. The crew could see Waimea as William Ellis of the *Resolution* had painted it thirteen years before: a cluster of rocks in the sea from which they must keep their distance, a river barely breaching its bar, a deep high-sided valley that forked north and south. For Hergest it was a familiar place to water but, by all the rules he should have learned of contact with Pacific peoples, not particularly safe. The watering party would be out of sight and the ship would be an hour away from help. Hergest was about to commit the last imprudent act of a fairly imprudent life.

Hergest was an impetuous young man and, it has to be said, a miserable young man at this time. The Admiralty had joined in their minds Vancouver's expedition to the northwest coast and the new penal settlement at Botany Bay ten thousand miles away. They saw the *Daedalus* as their line of communication. Hergest believed there was a good chance that he would spend long years either in the desolate North American trading place, or in the bleak penal colony at the end of the earth, or plying between these two uncivilized posts. He had wept copious tears on the voyage out. He did not cope well with his poor prospects or with his peculiar position as the only naval man on a trading ship.

Stripped of all the supportive paraphernalia of navy discipline, he did not prove to be a successful commander. There had been much insubordination and quarrelling on the voyage, and as they approached Waimea the crew were distracted by their own venal interest in making profit out of trade for Hawaiian artifacts. As they anchored and prepared to send a cutter ashore to get water, there was a violent scene on the deck. Hergest was shoving overboard the Hawaiians who had clambered aboard to trade, shouting at his sailors to go about their business, and then angrily demanding that the watering crew go ashore unarmed.

Why he insisted the men be unarmed is difficult to understand. Perhaps he thought that by this there would be no temptation for the Hawaiians to steal weapons. Perhaps he knew from his experience at Kealakekua that the Hawaiians would not collect water for the ship unless they were paid in arms once they saw them. When the mate and some of the crew refused to obey his orders, Hergest turned to William Gooch and four sailors with whom Hergest was friendly and asked them to come with him. As they prepared to go, the captain (who was aboard representing the owner) and some of the sailors secreted weapons on board the cutter. Among the weapons was a musketoon, hard to hide. Maybe Hergest turned a blind eye.

William Gooch's own relations with Hergest were strained. On that strange little ship, the young Gooch, twenty-one years old and totally inexperienced, and the older Hergest–who was all of thirty-seven years and on his third voyage to the Pacific with more than twenty years in the navy–formed an intense friendship that frequently blew apart and mended with their changing moods. Just a day or two before at Kealakekua, they had seemed to quarrel irretrievably. Gooch, expecting to join Vancouver soon as astronomer was threatened by Hergest with a report

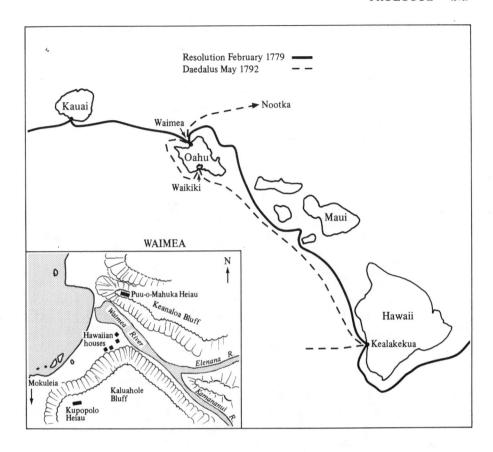

FIGURE 2: TRACKS OF THE *RESOLUTION* AND THE *DAEDALUS*,
HAWAIIAN ISLANDS; WAIMEA (inset).

of his negligence and disobedience that would ruin his career before it
was begun. Who can say what was in Hergest's mind when he turned to
Gooch and asked him to go ashore or why Gooch accepted? It would be
a good guess that they both saw an opportunity to pull their relationship
out of its trough and start it to another peak. They needed to talk and
be alone.

The first thing they did when they landed was to leave two sailors in
the boat where it had beached and two others at the watering place
where the river was especially sweet and deep. Then they walked off
alone up the river between the high cliffs. The last sight of them was of
their preoccupation with one another, talking, strolling, tri-cornered hats
together. With the strangeness of the place about to descend upon them,
they were in no strange place at all.

Had Hergest ears to hear aboard the *Daedalus*, he would have sensed the strangeness of Waimea. A young Hawaiian boy, who had a few words of English because he had been on a trader to China, begged him not to go ashore at Waimea. There were no chiefs, he said, and evil people resided there. An old man who had been full of bawdy gestures about Hawaiian women suddenly fell silent and melancholy as he saw that they insisted on landing. He saw his own life caught up in what was to follow. Indeed when it was all over and the *Daedalus* had retreated thirty miles to sea, the old man threw himself overboard still wearing the dead Hergest's greatcoat.

Hergest and Gooch were perhaps a mile up the river when Franklin, one of the sailors at the watering place, looked up to the bluff above him and saw Hawaiians clambering down with daggers in their hands and with obvious aggressive intent. They had their wildness stamped on their bodies. They were 'cut-in-two' by the bizarre pattern of their tattoos. Half of the body precisely, from head to toe, was tattooed totally black, or all of the head was tattooed except, so it was said, the teeth and the insides of the eyelids. These *pahupu* caught Manuel halfway along the beach. Franklin broke away, ran strongly through more Hawaiians coming from a different direction and made the boat. The weapons in the boat and their own small numbers made little difference. Straight away two of the crew went back along the beach and there found Manuel's naked battered corpse. A crowd of Hawaiians stood menacingly between them and Hergest and Gooch, who could now be seen in the distance in the midst of a shouting, gesticulating mob. It was dusk. There was nothing to be done but to return to the *Daedalus*, which itself had to stand off to sea the whole night long.

Hawaiians of a later date remembered what happened and told its story:

> A couple of foreigners went along the bank of the river. The two foreigners on the bank were killed. Said men walked along to where there was a large crowd then the natives decided to attack them. The natives threw rocks at them. One of the men was named Kapaleaiuku. He threw a rock which struck a foreigner on the jaw and he fell.
>
> And when the men on the other bank saw the white man had fallen, they all ran to this bank and beat the foreign men. The natives beat them, and said white men cried out because they were injured. A native said, "Say, they are groaning, perhaps they are human. And we thought they were gods because of their sparkling eyes." The natives kept beating them. A certain man said, "Say, be careful how you beat them. That's Lonoikaouali'i, a god. Lono died on Hawaii, Lonoikaoualii is the

one left here. This is big, strong, Pekeku, a god." The two white men were beaten to death. The people who were floating their water casks all ran to the opposite bank of the stream; they ran till they reached their boats then moved seaward. When the natives arrived the foreigners boarded their boats, sailed a short way, and in a little while fired their guns. They didn't flee; they merely floated quietly farther out.

And those on board the vessel looked ashore and saw that some of their men were dead. They turned their vessel broadside toward Waimea and fired their ship's guns. The natives exclaimed, "What is that reverberating sound?" Someone said, "I thought it was sand, but it was a death dealing thing; it may light up and everything will be destroyed. We probably will be saved because these two gods have died or they would have stayed and all of us would have been killed." There was gunfire from that vessel all through the day till night and then it disappeared.

1

ARTIFICIAL CURIOSITIES

There are lives caught like dried flowers between the pages of a book. I would not like this life of William Gooch to be like that–exemplary, still. Now that I have found him, I wish him resurrection for who he was, not just for how I would use him. But his life has no monument other than this book, and by that it is joined to my purposes, my artificial curiosities.

In any case, there is in history no resurrection. There is only cultivated meaning, although our common prejudice is otherwise. History, by that prejudice, is not an artificial curiosity at all. History, by common sense, is the past itself. It is independent of our knowing, as wild as reality, controlled and ordered like life, perhaps, but not by us.

I have no desire to be absurdist or deconstructionist. I am not intent on making a jungle of history's enchanting garden. I know the lethargy that too much reflection creates. I happily kick the stone with Dr. Johnson to mock Bishop Berkley's idealism. In this history of the death of William Gooch, I simply offer an ethnographic reflection. I owe William Gooch–because of the pleasure he has given me in discovering him–the realism of a crafted story, an ethnography of his life. I owe him presence in the ways of life he actually experienced. But I am a product of my times as much as he was of his. The realism I crave for him is crafted too–by my ironies, by my show of doubt as well as certainty, by display of exhaustive research, by all the tropes that persuade you that he not I is present. At this moment too, how can I pretend that Roland Barthes, Michel Foucault and Victor Turner have not spoken or that Marshall Sahlins has not written *Historical Metaphors and Mythical Realities*? Ethnography now with no reflection is no ethnography at all.

My ethnographic reflection on the death of William Gooch is called *History's Anthropology*. By the ambivalences that apostrophes create, *History's Anthropology* comprises at the one time the anthropology of history, historical anthropology, and anthropological history. But not the history of anthropology! Whatever else *History's Anthropology* might be, in the death of William Gooch it explores the ways in which history is both a metaphor of the past and a metonymy of the present.

Let me explain that gnomic thought. Once, in the middle of a scholastic disputation on the nature of the divine, I heard a theology professor, frustrated at our botched efforts to emulate both the wisdom and the lucid latin of Thomas Aquinas, exclaim "God is the eternal

Nunc." "God is the eternal Now."

An eternal *Nunc* is a cosmological tease for us mortals. We who live in time cannot catch a present but that it is gone in the catching of it. Our experiential world is all interpretation in the moment-after of its stimulus. These stimuli–these sights and sounds and feelings–are gone and we are left with a memory instantly made, a meaning constructed of them, a sign of them caught in some artifact. Our pasts suffuse our presents in this transformed, translated, interpreted, encapsulated way.

Let me call these pasts suffusing our presents in this transformed, translated, interpreted, encapsulated way, History. Perhaps you have come to know that history is something different: history is something that one writes or learns; history is a science or an art. Perhaps for you history is what really happened–the poor exploited, the colonized degraded, hegemony extended. Let us not argue over what History ought to be. Let us flourish our commitments later. The History of my artificial curiosity is a universal phenomenon. History is all the ways we encode the past in symbol form to make a present. It is in this sense very vernacular. It is an everyday, every moment act. Making History is our constant cultural exercise. We express the past and by that make our social relations and our social structures. We make boundaries of class, of sex, of age or role in our constant History making. We create change, we establish the status quo in our History making.

Perhaps in identifying History with the cultural process itself we have cast our net too wide. In saying History is everything, we have said nothing. So let me refine the idea a little. History is the texted past for which we have a cultural poetic. It is in that sense not all experience but that part of it which is transformed into texts–texts written down, texts spoken, texts caught in the forms of material things. We might, if we tried, make some typology of these texts–gossip, family anecdote, sailor's yarns, sacred history, historical monograph–based on their different social occasions. We might make some typology across different systems of cultural signs–Hawaiian, say, or 18th century English. There are histories, different modes of the texted past. There is History, an analytic concept whose common character histories shape.

These texts of the past are public. They are available to be read, heard, seen, interpreted. They are not locked away in personal, undisplayed memory. History is not just personal memory unless it is that personal memory made artifact, external, social, cultural.

Histories differ. We learn to read or hear them variedly. With one or another, we are adept at applying the appropriate poetic. Each text has its cultural and social system for being read. Take gossip about something that has happened. Gossip is a text crafted with many signals of confidence and conspiracy, highlighted with a glance to see if somebody is listening, phrased to titillate with the most savory or unsavory bit reserved for the ending. One could not divorce the inflections of voice, the body posture, the signs of intimacy from all the techniques of story-telling in a gossip's performance of history. We who hear the gossip have a fine sense of its poetics as we separate the snide from the good-humored, commit ourselves or suspend our judgement of its truth, know what friendly relations are damaged or enhanced by it. We produce histories by performing them and we live by being critics of their theatre.

We are socialized and acculturated to our variety of histories. We move easily between them with no sense of contradiction. We discipline ourselves with accuracy in academic history. We embellish the mythic truth of stories to our children with fantasy. Expression about the past in histories is crafted: it is gossip, it is diary, it is birth certificate, it is monument, and inscription, it is *History's Anthropology*.

The reading of this crafted expression is always systematic. The freedom to read it as one likes is always licensed by a common sense of what meanings the expression will bear, what ambivalences it will cover, in what way our readings will distinguish the text from the past of which it is the transformation.

If it is true that there is no past in the present–not even that which happened a breath or a blink ago–that is not texted and crafted, then it is also true that there is no texted and crafted past in the present that is not archived by some system of preservation. The texted past is always preserved in some way. It does not continue by accident. It sometimes disappears by accident but it is always preserved systematically. In being preserved these texts are re-textualized with added value and meaning. The pasts of kings and chiefs are textualized by their preservation differ-ently from the past of commoners, and men from women, and literate from illiterate. We who have such complex poetics for reading the texted past have poetics as well for its systems of preservation.

So the raw experience of the past is parcelled into texts. These texts are parcelled in their turn by the institutions that preserve them. Histo-rians exploring the past come across it in highly cultivated clearings. But we all, by being cultured, have a kit of different poetics to read the texted, re-texted past. Our application of these poetics is so ordinary and easy an act that we do not have a word to describe it. To borrow one from Victor Turner, we can call it entertainment.

Now "entertain" might seem to be a frivolous word to be used in so serious a subject. The texted past, after all, creates too much pain in the present, the texted past is too engrained in our existential being to think that our reading of it is just play. But words have meaning in their usage, not in their substance. Entertainment comes ultimately from the latin *inter tenere* "to hold among or between." Of the sixteen dictionary usages of the word "entertain" only one usage is devoted to the frivolous or amusing element in it. All the other usages stress its active, defining quality: "to keep in a certain state," "to support," "to engage, keep occupied the attention of," "to harbour," "to take upon oneself." Entertaining a thought or entertaining a guest has a boundary-making, dramaturgical character. If I entertain a guest I put all sorts of boundary markers around our host/guest relationship. I do things with extravagant gesture, out of the ordinary. I place my guest at table, I dress carefully, I formalize the menu, I use special utensils, I move the conversation away from sensitive issues. I play the role of host in a thousand small ways and the guest responds as dramatically. Our host/guest relationship is *presented* in dramatic actions.

In History past and present are similarly indivisible. Performances about the past in History *are* the present. In History too, performers are not really divisible from the audience: gossip, the text of the story, is not really divisible from gossiping, the context in which the story is told. Sacred scripture as artifact, as book, establishes relationships of deference and awe at the altar, but poetics of indifference in a hotel room. Sacred scripture as text, as History, cannot be divorced from its reading which, public or private, gives context to the expression of meaning. The performance of sacred scripture in some structuralist analysis of the Book of Genesis is very different from the performances of the same sacred scripture at an Easter Service. The performances entertain to different meanings: the performances constitute different presents, and the same person, structuralist and believer, might perform the same sacred scripture in different circumstances and feel no contradiction in being so relativist in his or her poetics.

The Past and the Other are two of humanity's main preoccupations. Rendering significant what has happened is a daily, seasonal, celebratory, generational activity, done in private and in public, personally and institutionally. Marking the boundaries of difference constantly defines self, role, class, culture. It divides young and old, living and dead, human and divine, native and stranger. No one, individually, socially, culturally is without a signified Past or a signified Other. But both the Past and the Other are more than present. They are pre*sented*—they are *pre*sented in the dramaturgies of our inventions. It is my "artificial curiosity" to ask how do I write history as if that were true?

2

MAKING HISTORY

Crafted Experience

By any measure of events that change the course of human development or exemplify great movement in human thought, the death of William Gooch was and is of no great importance. But the deaths of Gooch, Hergest and Manuel made History in the ways History is always made, by the selective transformations of events and experiences into public cultural forms of narrative. The Hawaiians and British told stories to themselves and each other about what happened. Those stories as History had different forms–ritual chant, triumphant song, official explanation, anecdote, gossip, condolence, evidence in a court of inquiry, answers to queries about the Hawaiian "People of Old." Those who heard the stories were entertained by them. They knew the History not just in the words of the stories but in the form of their expression and the occasion of their telling.

The first story of the death of William Gooch and the others came from a survivor of the killings, the sailor named Franklin who ran back along the beach through the attacking Hawaiians. He told the boat crew at the water's edge that he had shouted a warning to Manuel that an "Indian" was running toward him with a drawn dagger. Hergest and Gooch, a mile or more away, could not be warned, though they must have seen the frantic bustle as women fled their houses and men moved their canoes inland. The boat crew went back along the beach with Franklin, found the bloodied corpse of Manuel and saw Hergest and Gooch in the distance in the midst of a crowd of clamoring Hawaiians. It was dusk. The sailors were poorly armed and more than two hundred Hawaiians stood threateningly near. So they returned to the *Daedalus*, three miles out to sea.

On the *Daedalus* the stories of what happened on shore were translated into stories of what "really" happened. In their double distance from the events the *Daedalus's* crew read the signs of fear or cowardice or self-interest or ineptitude encoded in the words of the boat crew's stories. They reformulated these stories with hints and silences and euphemisms so that we learn from the re-telling not just more about the unpredictability of savages, but something about the imprudence of Hergest and Gooch in going ashore unarmed and out of sight of the ship, the courage and resoluteness of the English sailor, Franklin, and the spiritual weakness of the foreigner Portuguese seaman in not fighting for his life.

The crew collapsed time in their stories as they made what happened before and after the killings significant for understanding them. They embellished their narratives with the hindsight of all that had happened on the voyage. The tensions they had endured as a merchant crew with Hergest as lone naval commander now made sense, as did the silly quarrel he had with the first mate just minutes before going ashore at Waimea. They had seen Hergest's rash rages the whole voyage long and they had seen his rashness again as he pushed an Hawaiian angrily over-board because the watering had been delayed by unofficial trading. The *Daedalus's* crew now remembered that the old Hawaiian on board and the young Hawaiian who spoke little English had both warned Hergest not to go ashore because the people of Waimea were evil and there were no chiefs. Hergest had not listened.

They could tell in their stories how they sailed out to sea that night and on returning next morning found the Hawaiians on the beach gloating and making taunts, capering about in Hergest's cockade hat and Gooch's clothing. They had fired their cannon and muskets till the "Indian" who had shown the greatest bravado fell, and they knew they were rescued from judgement against their own savage, revengeful slaughter by what would be seen to be the irrational intransigence of savages.

So they crafted their experience into small dramas—out of signs of reality hidden behind living words, they made today's experience make sense of yesterday's. They joined past to present. They told their stories to themselves for the camaraderie it gave in shared concern, in protested innocence. They told the stories to others, piecemeal and in different ways, to other ships on the northwest coast, to the crews of Vancouver's *Discovery* and *Chatham* when they met up with them. They told their stories for the rest of their lives in pubs and ships. Sailors' yarns are famous. Like joking relationships and gossip, they need an anthropology. Who among us does not display class, sex, or person in stories about something Other? And who among us in reading stories about something Other does not read something else?

Texted Past

The stories of the *Daedalus* were gone on the breath of their speech. The Past is always as evanescent, except when it is made into the kind of artifact that the *Daedalus's* crew made by writing their experiences down. Captain Thomas New, we might suppose, was the first to do so. His was the responsibility, now that Hergest was gone, to enter the events in the *Daedalus's* log. That he did so we know because Vancouver in his official published account quotes Captain New's story out of the *Daedalus's* log. Indeed there were several officers of the great cabin of the *Discovery* who were confident that they knew the true history of these events because they had been privileged to read the *Daedalus's* log.

The authenticity of a witness is magnified by the witness's official status and the testimony's encoded form. Every officer read the log in a knowing way for the meaning in and behind the words, for what was not said at all, for the system in its preservation. Every officer knew, because they were practiced in it, what sort of public history a log might be, and how different it was to other more private histories. Indeed for the scandal they wanted to reveal, for the intrigue of being an insider to another past, they made other private histories, in letters or journals tucked away from official scrutiny.

There is not much to be said of the epistemology of Captain New's log because all we have of it are citations from it. We do not know if Captain New made his own log or if, more probably, he was sensitive to the proprieties of succession and continued Hergest's log. The official papers of the *Daedalus* were handed to Vancouver in any case. Yet, strange to say for a man of such public discovery, Vancouver's personal papers have not been seen since his premature death and his brother's publication of his account of his *Voyage of Discovery*.

Vancouver counted Hergest as his most "intimate friend." They had been midshipmen together on Cook's fatal third voyage. There has to be a faint suspicion that in the pain of loss there was a sense of protection of the dead Hergest's reputation. The Past is secured by destroying it as well as shaping it.

There were other ways in which the past of Hergest and Gooch (not really of Manuel) was texted. Their companions wrote testimonies to courts of inquiry, identifying the guilt of natives and the unpredictability of savages, blurring the imprudence of officers, hiding their own venal interests. They wrote letters to the bereaved parents of Gooch, saying there was no meaning to the events except in divine providence. They wrote gossiping letters making these side issues of a voyage of discovery centrally significant to their picture of Vancouver's bungling authoritarianism. They registered the events for bureaucratic institutions–the precise time of death in both naval and civilian time so the lawyers could calculate to the penny wages due to the dead, the price got from the auction of dead men's clothes, the list of properties privately and publicly owned. Neither birth nor death are so private that institutions do not own some part of them. Law, Church, State, Navy, and the Board of Longitude in attending to Gooch, parcelled his life into bits of texted pasts. These pasts on paper were tidied, collected, indexed, archived to institutional memory. Who could count the vested interests of successive Presents in keeping that Past so ordered? It is not like living with the eternal compromise between order and process. The Past was boxed by the blinkered questions that institutions asked as they made and deposited their records.

Then there were more private stories, when the blaze of public concern had died down. These gave a detail, saying that Hergest's real anger had been with the whole *Daedalus's* crew because they had refused to stop trading for Hawaiian curiosities that would make them a small fortune and denied him help in watering the ship for the common good. Years after the event they wrote stories, notes in the margins of printed accounts that vented their old jealousies and anger, autobiographical accounts and memorials that leached their own lives to the nodal points of their famous occasions. And twenty, thirty, even fifty years later not just they, the witnesses or near-witnesses, but those who joined themselves to the events by discovering a witness or hearing of an irony from one witness to another inscribed the story again or gave it another ending.

There is a word describing such reconstitution of meaning that has been appropriated with special significance in Pacific studies. It is "cargo." Cargo consists of cultural material things that come across a beach. Cargo is an artifact of another culture. It might be an iron adze, a bible, a musket. Within any culture an artifact is a manifold text of values, of systems, of perceptions and relations. Beauty, the means and relations of production, ownership and exchange, and morality are written into the cultural things we have in hand. In the context of our culturally-given signs and symbols we read the meanings encapsulated in our things. Where things cross a cultural boundary we re-invent their meanings. The Hawaiians and the *Daedalus's* crew exchanged curiosities across their different cultural boundaries. The *Daedalus's* crew re-invented what they received, made icons and weapons into saleable collector's pieces. Collectors and museum visitors would read these goods as signs of savage Otherness. How could they read them for what they were–things that bound men to gods, separated men from women, chiefs from commoners? And how could their readings be sacramental of their meaning, *actually* binding men to gods, separating men from women, chiefs from commoners? The new readings were sacramental of other meanings, of the class and status of collectors, of the superiority of the civilized over savages. The Hawaiians were as inventive. Re-shaping the strangers' goods to their own functions, they were also re-shaped a little by things over whose production and introduction they had little or no control.

There are boundaries in time as well as space, between Past and Present as well as Native and Stranger. The texted Past is inevitably cargo to successive Presents. The Past made artifact in a text has continuity that its evanescent context of symbols and readings can never have. The texted Past is always beached in Presents that always re-invent it. It is never absolutely within the time of one culture: there is a joining as well as a division between Past and Present. But be wary of those who claim to understand this double helix of now and then.

Texting the Past–and by that making History–is always one-sided and selective. Having a Von Rankean ambition or even an ethnographic one to describe "what actually happened" becomes difficult when the same event is possessed in culturally different ways. Both the British and the Hawaiians made history of the death of William Gooch. It takes something of an eternal *Nunc* to claim that the past of neither is what actually happened, but that it is what we invent from our vantage point. In vain do the ghosts of Gooch and Hergest peer over our shoulder and say "but we were there." The Past is never likely to recognize itself in History, any more than natives are likely to recognize themselves in ethnography.

Collapsed Time

The Hawaiians made their History of the deaths of Gooch and Hergest, too. What that History immediately was we can only surmise out of what it later was. This is not a different procedure to that we have been following in describing the histories made by the European stranger. It is complicated by the fact that the histories the Hawaiians made were–to use Lévi-Strauss's metaphor–'cooked' or at least heated by the contact that made Hawaiian native and European stranger environmental to one another. We see Hawaiian-made History in the first instance only through the looking glass of strangers' eyes.

Independent of everything else, Hawaiians made History of the deaths by sacrificing Hergest and Gooch. They took the bodies to a *heiau* ('temple'), cooked them and divided them among Oahu chiefs. They themselves said the *heiau* was at Mokuleia, about twelve miles along the coast to the west. European interpreters of Hawaiian history, wishing it to be more commonsensical, suggest that the *heiau* might have been Puu-O-Mahuka at Waimea itself. But one man's commonsense is another man's mystery. If there was a reason to take the victims to Mokuleia, or if there was a reason for making History as if the bodies were taken specially to Mokuleia then we do not know it.

Sacrifice was not necessarily the purpose of what was done. Hergest and Gooch were not necessarily killed because they were wanted as victims. Sacrifice made sense of what had already been done. Sacrifice was History. The British had a suspicion, no doubt born of a feeling of guilt at having deserted Gooch and Hergest, that the two were not killed in the *mêlée* but had been killed in the early hours of the next morning. But the Hawaiians did not make of their sacrifice a dramaturgic killing, biblically appropriate though that might have been. They were interested more in the killed than in the killing, although they had their prejudices, too. They never sacrificed Manuel, only Gooch and Hergest.

There were rubrics to be observed, nonetheless. The bodies were to be stripped and bound and cleaned. The hair was to be cut, the eyes scooped out, the penis mutilated and the testicles exposed. Ordinarily the immolated body rotted on the altar, but to speed the division of the bones it might be cooked. The gods' share was burned. The skull and jaw, the hair and long bones were distributed to chiefs in the order of their status.

I have not the knowledge to decode all these gestures and symbols. I am a borrower on these points from Valerio Valeri and Marshall Sahlins. Nor have I the space to define more precisely the possibilities, probabilities and certainties of what happened to Hergest and Gooch after their death. I would wish only to score the point that the Hawaiians, in making History of the deaths of Gooch and Hergest by sacrificing them, transformed whoever they saw them to be into victims. By that they displayed their distinctions of power and authority, they divided commoner and chief, land and sea, native and stranger. In their History they entertained themselves as to who they really were. And, of course, they made of the bones of their victims documents for the archives of their temples, as artifactual as a letter or a book.

As it happened, the Hawaiians made History in their sacrifices in a special place at Waimea. Puu-o-Mahuka was the largest *heiau* of all Oahu. It stood on top of the northern bluff (see Figure 8). It was a place of sacrifice. The *Daedalus's* crew could have seen it from three miles out to sea. Manuel could have seen it as he watered the casks under the southern bluffs. From the direction of Puu-o-Mahuka had come the *pahupu* who killed Gooch and Hergest.

Waimea was a place of priests. The whole of Waimea had belonged to priestly classes for generations. In 1792 it belonged to the *kahuna alii*, a class of priestly chiefs. Their representative at that time was a remarkable man called Koi, remarkable in his bizarre appearance, remarkable in his familial connections. As *pahupu*, Koi was a member of a military cohort who wore their insignia tattooed on their skin. Even in the hyperbole of Hawaii's extravagant warrior code, *pahupu* were reputed to be wild. *Pahupu* fought for Kahekili. Kahekili was chief of Maui, a rival, in his last years of life, to Kamehameha for hegemony over all the Hawaiian islands.

For ten years Kahekili had ruled Oahu as well as Maui, leaving his son as governor at Waikiki. While the focus of his struggle with Kamehameha remained on Maui and Hawaii, Kahekili had left Koi at Waimea. It was a rebellious and restless area.

Koi was soldier. He was also sacrificing priest. He had inherited his place at Waimea from his father, Kaleopuupui. Kaleopuupui was the brother of Kaopulupulu, the quintessential "pestilential priest" of the Hawaiian islands. At a later time, fifty years after these events at Waimea, Kaopulupulu was remembered for his martyr's death. In that memory he was Thomas à Beckett to Waimea's King Henry, Kahana. Kaopulupulu was remembered for being murdered by Kahana when the priest warned the chief about ceding sacred land to Kahekili. That sacred land was proof of Kahana's legitimate authority. Kaopulupulu made a pact with his son to die. "Take a deep breath and give your body to the sea. The land is the sea's," he said. He himself was then killed on the beach, between land and sea. It was mythic History he was making. He called on deep metonymies to sustain it. "Land"–legitimate authority, native people, nurturing force–was being possessed by "sea"–usurping power, violence, strangers from afar. In the later memory, his History was seen as prophecy. Native Hawaii would be possessed by European strangers.

I have begun to condition all I say by referring to a later memory. In this archeology of knowledge all the relics of the past have been leached from the sequence of their deposit and are shown to be lying on the surface of experience. I make sense of Kaopulupulu's History/prophecy because of what Sahlins has written about the opposition in Hawaii between Land and Sea, Native and Stranger, People and Chief. I cannot escape the sentences he has written when I read the sentences Hawaiians have written about themselves. The Hawaiians themselves could not escape their own collapse of time. Their past of 1782-1792 was conjoined with their present of 1838 when it was inscribed in their written-down History. The Past that I confront in making History of Hawaiian Natives and European Strangers making History is out of specific time. It is processually cultural. It is public, systematic. We can see its structures. But it includes its own changes.

Hawaiians began to read and write in the early 19th century. It was a revolution as culturally spontaneous as the overthrow of the *kapu*, but also as conditioned by the environment of Stranger contact in which it happened. In 1841 the Royal Hawaiian Historical Association was formed. It was an "Association for the conserving of historical data concerning the chiefs of Hawaii and Kauai, the origin of their race, their

first ancestors, their first chiefs, their first servants, the first men who
sailed to Kahiki, the first men of Kahiki who came here, the first
foreigners who came to the islands, the first ships, etc." "If we do not
gather these data now," it was said at the time, "after many generations
our children would be like American Indians–a race without history."

The Royal Hawaiian Historical Association itself had begun five years
earlier when Sheldon Dibble, a missionary, collected the ten best
scholars of the missionary seminary at Lahainaluna. In discussion with
them, Dibble established a series of questions which they then individually asked the oldest and most knowing of the chiefs and people. They
committed what they learned to writing, read it to the class, reconciled
discrepancies and gave the accounts to Dibble to form one corrected
version.

One of the students, Samuel Kamakau, was inspired to continue his
inquiries for twelve years. He published them in the Hawaiian language
newspapers then blossoming in the literary revolution. He remembered
later that the start of his searching was motivated by a desire to discover
an independent Hawaiian antiquity which he saw slighted by foreign
history that described Hawaiians as a wandering lost race, or a remnant
of American Indians, or a people spawned in some volcanic eruption. He
was possessed of ambitions that in the end were never fulfilled. He
would "cover thoroughly the islands." "There were no more people
conversant with old history," he wrote. "Those who are left are trying to
make out that they are beacon lights of historical subjects. The
foreigners only know so much and they are superficial!...History is of
great value when founded on facts for it becomes a word resting on a
foundation."

Kamakau became a Roman Catholic convert and in the politics of
knowledge was teased by the tensions and visions Catholicism gave him.
He had, as well, suspicions of the British, born of his American Lahainaluna education. He was also ambivalent about chiefs, as he came to learn
in his own life the contradictions of power and authority. It was his story
of the death of Gooch that collapsed the time of the European coming
and the Hawaiian's mythic understanding of themselves into a dialectic
of Native People and Stranger Chiefs. It was he who made of Kaopulupulu's cry, "The land is the sea's," a prophecy (see Figure 3).

Inevitably the Hawaiian histories were inclusive of earlier and later
experiences and all that happened in-between. So their History of the
death of Gooch was inclusive of their History of the death of Cook.
Cook, they knew, was to be blamed for his own death. He had willingly
played the part of a god, had willingly entered their myths and by that
had played them out in his body. Hergest and Gooch were innocent of
such an intrusion. Their killing was senseless. Mythic perception of them
as gods, as Lonoikouali'i, was one-sided, Hawaiian. These Strangers had

FIGURE 3: JOHN WEBBER'S 1778 WATERCOLOR OF AN HAWAIIAN *HEIAU* AT WAIMEA ON THE ISLAND OF *KAUAI*.

The Land is the Sea's: Kamakau's History of the Waimea Priest. Ka-'opulupulu was living on his lands in Waimea and I'upukea when Ka-hahana went around Oahu with the chiefs, counselors, guards, *kahunas*, and attendants, and restored the most important *heiaus*, observed strictly the tabus on the *heiaus*, and ate of the fat of the land. At Wai'anae he restored the *heiau* of Ka-moho-ali'i and sent for Ka-'opulupulu. When the messenger came to him at Waimea the *kahuna* [Ka-'opulupulu] said, "Tell the chief that we two will come tomorrow." The next day he and his only son, Ka-hulu-pue, set out, and when they reached Ka-ananiau at Ka-ena Point he said to his son, "Let us pray that we may know whether this journey is for good or evil." When he had prayed he said, "The gods show me that we shall die. Here is the way leading to life, and here is the way leading to death." The son chose the road to life. The father said, "If we take the road you have chosen we shall not gain vengeance in this world, but if we die we shall be avenged. The chief shall die, his dominion shall be taken, and none of his offspring shall survive. It is better for us to take the road to death." The son consented. When they reached Wai'anae Ka-hahana at once ordered that Ka-hulu-pue be put to death. The *kahuna* called out to his son, "Take a deep breath and give your body to the sea; the land is the sea's!" The boy ran and dived into the sea of Malae and died there. Then the chiefs and the commoners, hearing of Ka-hulu-pue's death, were uneasy in their minds, but Ka-hahana paid no attention to his counselors' words, and when they reached Pu'uloa Ka-'opulupulu was killed. The leading counselor of the island being thus dead the people lost courage, for the foundation of the dominion was shaken.

made no gestures, no signs that they were any other than outsiders. They were not mythic Strangers at all. So their killing was cruel and belonged to the politics of chiefs. "The land mourned the blood of men shed without cause, because of the pride and arrogance of the chiefs who desired to get land and riches at the sacrifice of human blood. Let the Hawaiians ponder these things," wrote Kamakau.

What the Hawaiians might ponder upon was that the chiefs were living out their myths despite themselves. They might walk on the Land, like sharks, but senseless sacrifice would be their end, as it had been the end of Kahahana, the murderer of Kaopulupulu; as it had been the end of Kahekili. They might kill strangers for their guns. They might kill their native people with guns wrested from strangers. In the end there would be other sharks, "and the line of chiefs would end, and a stubborn generation would succeed them who would cause the native race to dwindle."

See how the Hawaiians entertained themselves with their History of the death of Gooch.

Readings as Theatre

George Vancouver was a didactic man of large gestures. When he learned of the death of Hergest and Gooch he returned to Hawaii bent on teaching the Hawaiians the significance of what had happened. He was bent on making sacrifice to law and justice. He came—he said it often—to let the "Indians" see that long after the event and at inconceivable distances from the sources of power, abstract justice could reach out even to individuals responsible for an injust killing. He wanted to make a theatre of guilt, of impartial justice, of evidence and reason, of impersonal judgement, of punishment. He thought public executions made excellent History.

Vancouver enters most of our histories as the seventeen-year-old midshipman who climbed to the end of the bowsprit of the *Resolution* when Cook had taken his ship as far to the south as he could go, to 72° South latitude. "*Ne plus ultra*," the young Vancouver shouted. And he boasted forever after that he had gone further south than any other man. But History is always quisling to such claims. Andreas Sparrman, the Swedish physician aboard the same ship, hurried down to the great cabin and caught the sternway as the ship began to tack, to catch a few feet further south. Both stories, told with a boast or an ironic chuckle, no doubt repeated often, entertained tellers and hearers to different histories of the same symbolic act.

Of course, as a history professor I might have said—I have said—"Cook reached further south than any other man to that date." Cook himself thought he did:

> I will not say it was impossible anywhere to get in among this ice, but I will assert that the bare attempting of it would be a very dangerous enterprise and what I believe no man in my situation would have thought of. I whose ambition leads me not only farther than any other man has been before me but as far as I think it possible for man to go, was not sorry at meeting with this interruption, as it in some measure relieved us from the dangers and hardships, inseparable with the navigation of the southern polar regions. Since therefore we could not proceed one inch farther south, no other reason need be assigned for our tacking and stretching back to the north, being at that time in the Latitude 71°10' South, Longitude 106°54' West.

The man really farthest south in Cook's story was the man who made the decisions, the man whose ambition lead him as far as it was possible for man to go. His "*I*" encompassed all the others.

Such History is easily and often made. Those who went farthest south in a steamship, in a yacht, single-handed, as a female, as an American or Chilean or Frenchman, or just since the last voyager, made History, had their actions recorded, left their marks on something more permanent than a melting iceberg. Wherever these History-making records are kept and whoever keeps them, they shape the character of George Vancouver's story, of Sparrman's sly negating of it and Cook's lone reflection in his journal. The Past made Present in a story has a continually changing *double entendre* about something that is gone and about something that is made by the telling of it.

I cannot tell how often the midshipman-become-captain, Vancouver, told his story at the messtable to subordinates who were his captive audience for four years in the *Discovery*–very often, to judge by the groaning nostalgic tone of his obituary in which it was revealed. It would not be extraordinary if he told it so often that the audience knew its cadences, knew the cues that brought it on, could start it with a wink at one another. It would not be extraordinary, given the right conditions–a glass of port on some festival far from home, in some relaxation after a dangerous event–that the story was still engaging, that they indulged themselves with the familiarity it bred, that sometimes they could laugh at him in the telling, and sometimes laugh with him. The memory of it could be bitter. The memory of it could be sweet. Its facticity was long gone in importance. Rather, its facticity was continually changing with its audience and its narrator. Be wary of the history that claims to be separate from the circumstances of its telling or to have only one meaning.

George Vancouver was on the northwest coast of North America when the *Daedalus* brought news of Hergest's and Gooch's deaths. The northwest coast was becoming an edge of empire. When the *Resolution*, after Cook's death in Hawaii, made her way home by Canton in 1779, her crew discovered that the furs, especially the silken lush skin of the sea otter, which they had collected as curios, were worth a fortune on the Chinese market. They wanted then and there, almost to the point of mutiny, to turn around and try their trading luck.

Later a number of them did return in trading vessels and whalers. But then their fortunes were not so easily made, not because the furs were scarce or the Chinese disinterested, but because they did not reckon into the cost of their trading, their jealousies of one another and the possessiveness of empires and monopoly companies. Spain claimed territory all along the American continent from Cape Horn to Alaska and by that closed an eastern access to the Pacific. The British East India Company claimed a monopoly of all trade with China and closed by that a western entry to the Pacific. But claims and counter-claims to empire and monopoly needed some staging to be recognized. George Vancouver was sent to the Pacific to make a play of a peculiar kind of empire.

The Spaniards when they talked among themselves about empire used to say they really did not need more land: they just needed to be careful about their neighbors, the Russians first, then the British. The far reaches of the Spanish empire were the problem. Where there were forts and ports and settlements in San Francisco, Lima and Valparaiso the signs of possession could easily be read. Territoriality could be managed with civilized etiquette. Deferences and salutes to flag and authority could define the sort of presence foreigners might have and the sorts of privileges of food and comfort visitors might expect. Yet on the fringes of empire there was great ambivalence. At Nootka Sound there had been a series of troublesome events–confiscation of British trading vessels, conflicts about the public signs of settlement, imprisonment of foreigners. In 1790 Spain and Britain almost went to war. Spain, deserted by a France preoccupied with its revolution, capitulated. Vancouver's task was to go to Nootka and establish a peculiar sort of empire for Britain. It was not at that time to be an empire of territory. For territorial empires there were set signals–hoist a flag, turn a sod, give three cheers for his Britannic Majesty. All sorts of History had been made with these sets of signals. The eyes of other empires had been easily bent to see the History being made by them: "this bit of land belongs to us."

The British were interested in an empire of trade, of lines of communication, that would somehow supercede the empire of land. They had to be inventive of signs to make others see what they were about. In the end, well after Vancouver was gone, there was a strange little ceremony

at Nootka in which the British hoisted a flag to say they had a right to
be there, and then they pulled it down. Next the Spaniards and British
withdrew, similtaneously, careful not to be one before the other. Reifications are a problem when signs are seen only as symbols. But they are
much more a problem when eyes can see neither sign nor symbol.

It has to be said that George Vancouver came to Hawaii to enact
justice, confident that his theatre would be so full of natural signs that
any eye, even an "Indian's" eye, could see them. States and kings come
easily to symbols of power and sovereignty in a ceremonial killing. "All
grandeur, all power, all subordination rests on the executioner," De
Maistre had written at this time, "and he is the horror and the bond of
human associations. Remove this incomprehensible agent from the world
and at that very moment order gives way to chaos, thrones topple, and
society disappears." They could have been Vancouver's words.
Vancouver, in describing what he did, used a sort of hushed hyperbole,
as justice, awesome power, dignified acceptance of fate, responsible
authority and death itself stood revealed in the gestures, poses, words
and spaces of his ritual. He did not seem to notice that in the mad
margins between sets of symbols blind justice was something of a *poseur*.

Vancouver was very particular in his proprieties. He assembled his
officers as a court. He called witnesses under oath. He declared the
death sentences in solemn tones from the seat of his own authority, the
quarter-deck. By gestures of deference and dominance he delicately
balanced his own sovereignty and that of the chiefs. His rubrics were as
perfect as his rhetoric.

Making History by ritual always has its ambivalences. There is always
something to be seen in the occasion other than what the rubrics display.
Half a world away from Hawaii there were the twice yearly spectacles of
death on Tyburn Hill in London. The hangings were invested with all
the ceremonies of majesty that Vancouver wanted. The spectacle was
awesome–but the crowds were not always solemn. They came curious,
easily riotous, eager at times to get a sight of bodies and a touch of them
for the sickness it cured, happy to thwart the surgeons who wanted
corpses, buzzing for some resurrection that might come from the hang-
man's botched job. The language of the crowd was in no way hushed
hyperbole. They came to see a hanging match, a collar day, a Padding-
ton's Fair, a sheriff's ball, where a man might swing, or Morris, go west,
cry cockles, be robbed, backed, stretched, cheated, collared, nooged,
scragged, twisted, and "have a dry mouth and a pissin' pair of breeches."

Signs, by the making of them, are never certain. The texts of rituals
have the context of their reading. The text of Vancouver's ritual was
read in the context of the cynicism of his officers. They saw the shams
and the absurdities. While they made the signs work by their silent obeisance, they read in them an ugly view of their commander as well. The

Hawaiians, of course, were much freer to construct a meaning of Vancouver's signs all of their own.

From the distance of Nootka Sound, Vancouver's view of the death of Gooch and Hergest had been that a King of England's servant and commissioned officer had been killed in the polity of Hawaiian chiefs. He suspected that one of the two high chiefs warring for some hegemony over the islands was directly responsible. It would either be the young Kamehameha establishing himself on the large island of Hawaii or the old Kahekili on Maui but governing Oahu through his son Kalanikapule. One story Vancouver had heard was that Gooch and Hergest had been killed in retaliation for some offense a Captain Joseph Ingraham of the *Hope* had given the chiefs. If neither Kamehameha nor Kahekili were directly responsible, then they must be made to know their responsibilities as sovereign rulers.

On his arrival at Hawaii, however, Vancouver was easily persuaded by Kamehameha that the killings were none of his doing or responsibility. Kamehameha told him as well that his enemy Kahekili had already killed three of the murderers of Gooch and Hergest. After giving Kamehameha some civilized advice on the irrationality of war and the economic advantages of peace, Vancouver went on to Maui. There he immediately offended Kahekili by referring to Kamehameha as "high chief," the very point of their wars, but then mollified him with a gift of a scarlet robe with gold trappings. Kahekili assured Vancouver that the killings had been unprovoked and had been done by an unruly band, three of whom had been punished, four of whom were still at large on Oahu. Kahekili offered to send a chief, Kamohomohomo, with Vancouver to Oahu to identify the killers and bring them to punishment.

The governing of Oahu was not without its problems for Kahekili. There were indeed unruly bands on the island. They were concentrated in the lands of Waialua behind Waimea Bay. Koi, one of Kahekili's soldier chiefs, had led part of Kahekili's army in its invasion of Oahu. He had remained behind in the trouble area. As Kahekili's hopes of winning out against Kamehameha faded with Kamehameha's growing monopoly of European trade and weaponry, Kahekili had urged his soldiers to seize what weapons they could from trading vessels. Hence there was some ambiguity in the old Hawaiian's warning to Hergest on board the *Daedalus* concerning the wild people of Waimea. Was he referring to the people outside of Kahekili's control? Or were they like Koi, focussing their wildness on muskets and daggers? Whatever the old man's ambiguity, Kahekili had one of his own. He was not averse to removing unruly bands in the cause of justice.

At Oahu, Vancouver anchored off Waikiki, the residence of Kalanikapule, the governing chief. James Coleman, a beachcomber, came on board the *Discovery* together with Tahupuato the young Hawaiian with a little English who had been on the *Daedalus*. Tahupuato was clearly frightened by the role now given him of identifying the killers. He confirmed that Kahekili had had three men involved killed. He also said the killer of Gooch was still alive and lived in Waikiki. He promised to identify the other culprits with Coleman and return with them the next day. He never did. That was natural, the chiefs told Vancouver; he would fear the men's families.

The next morning the Maui chiefs came out to the *Discovery* in a large canoe and furtively identified three men sitting unconcernedly in it. The three men were seized and put in irons, much to their pleasure and not at all to their consternation. They were isolated from any Hawaiians or any Hawaiian-speaking crew who could tell them why they were being held. Vancouver formed his court-martial. The court was told to notice the tattooing of the three, one of whom was tattooed on half his body from forehead to feet. Coleman testified that he had heard that one of them had murdered Hergest but he could not speak for the other two. Later he swore under oath that Kalanikapule, absent all the time pleading illness, did not disagree with him. Thomas Dobson, a midshipman who had been on board the *Daedalus* and had seen "the insolent and improper behaviour of the native" when Hergest had pushed a man overboard pointed out the killer "without the least hesitation." He also backed his identification with an oath, but later more privately and out of court admitted his uncertainty. There was said to be a fourth man implicated. The Maui chiefs said he was not in the neighborhood. Vancouver agreed it would cost too much in time to go looking for him–and perhaps in prestige–if he were not found.

All the Maui chiefs, now impatient with the proceedings, wanted the executions then and there or, in some accounts, wanted Vancouver to sail out to sea and kill the accused men there. Vancouver gained confidence from the assurances of the chiefs but he wanted rather more obvious theatre. He decided to wait till next morning. He urged the chiefs to gather their people in canoes and ask anyone who had evidence of the men's innocence to come forward.

The next day there were noticeably fewer canoes and these moved away to a safe distance when Vancouver lined the decks with marines and rolled out the great guns facing them. Captain Simon Metcalf of the *Eleanora* had tricked and massacred Hawaiians in just that way a few years before.

The accused were brought out before the mainmast in front of the assembled officers and crew and the chiefs. They were given an opportunity to confess. They said they knew nothing of the killings. This was taken as evidence of their guilt. Who could know nothing of the killings?

Tennavee (Keawe?), a lesser chief of Waikiki, eagerly volunteered to be their executioner with a pistol. The first was bound and put face up in a canoe at the side of the *Discovery*. He gave Tennavee an "indignant look," said a few words as Tennavee put the pistol to his temple, and died without a groan. The second asked what had happened and "with manly firmness surrendered his existence." The third had a crest of flowing hair that might have impeded the pistol ball. So Vancouver ordered it cut off with scissors, and the chiefs squabbled and struggled over him each wanting to be the one to present the hair to Kalanika-pule. They had sacrifices of their own to make. When they had barbered him, he managed to fling himself overboard, bound hand and foot. He bobbed around in the water till they caught him and killed him like the others.

Vancouver wanted the bodies hung on a tree like a gibbet, but the chiefs said the priests would disapprove. Gibbets and altars are always in some competition. So the bodies were taken away in small canoes which paddled off "indifferently," it was said, yet the *Discovery* crew heard what they thought was a wailing when the canoes got further away.

Vancouver ordered a fireworks display that evening. He would not go ashore, however. Not, he wrote, because he thought the Hawaiians were hostile. Rather, because he would not tempt them. It was commonly agreed by Hawaiians and any European who enjoyed the irony that none of the men executed were guilty.

Through all the charades, Vancouver wanted to bend the gaze of the Hawaiians to the significance of what had happened. He wanted them to see that they had killed no ordinary men but naval officers touched in some way by a sovereignty and majesty greater than themselves. He wanted the Hawaiians to see Gooch's and Hergest's death decontextualized of their special circumstances, made universal by the inevitability of punishment. "Pusillanimous conduct on an occasion of this nature," he wrote with *realpolitik*, "could not fail to sink the character of Europeans into the lowest contempt." He specially wanted the chiefs to gain a sense of empire and its reaches; he wanted them to defer to his power and remain responsible for their own. So he talked to them in what he thought were universal symbols of power and authority—hushed silence, ponderous tones, military precision. Most of all he wanted them to see the signs by which the killers of Hergest and Gooch were transformed into sacrificial victims to order and law. In certain respects he expected this to be a self-transformation in which the victims made their obeisance, if not in confession then in deferring demeanor. He was pleased that the "melancholy office" of "blowing out their brains" was performed so "dextrously." "That life fled with the report of the piece and muscular motions seemed almost instantly to cease" was almost a reward for their manly composure. He was especially pleased that Tennavee was such a perfect executioner:

> If steadiness and firmness, totally devoid of the least agitation can be considered in the performance of such a duty as proof of conscious rectitude; or that the forfeiture of these three men's lives were considered as no more than what the strict principles of retributive justice demanded, it should be seen that Tennavee's mind had been completely made up, not only as judge, but as executioner; and that he was perfectly convinced his conduct was unimpeachable in executing an office that justice demanded.

We have to say that Tennavee did not think that way at all. The symbols he and the chiefs saw were their own, translated out of the Otherness of Vancouver's signs. There was ample evidence that both Vancouver's rhetoric and his rubrics passed them by–their impatience to be always doing something else, their distraction at their own exchanges. Vancouver read their squabbling and their preoccupation not as different or even as translated gestures, but as familiar signs of bad taste and impropriety. They were not Other, only bad-mannered. They participated in his rituals, but not properly.

We have to guess that they did participate in something else. In Maui's hegemony over Oahu? In sacrifice to Kalanikapule to whom the bodies of the executed were transported? In further legitimation of the division between *kapu* chiefs, the sacrificers, and commoners, the sacrificed? In the protective power of Maui chiefs for their soldier Koi?

And what of the Hawaiians who watched from their canoes? What History did they make of these Stranger and Native rituals bound together? We make guesses upon guesses. But Kamakau spoke for them a little. In his History he associated these events with the last days of Kahekili. His story was brief. It was a season of cruelty, a beginning of times of lawless people and lawless chiefs. It was not inappropriate that the killers of Gooch and Hergest were punished. It was not even inappropriate that Native authority should bow to Stranger power in their punishment. What was significant was that Kalanikapule of Waikiki and Kamohomohomo of Maui staged a fraud to protect their own close associates and sacrificed whoever was at hand. Dispossession was not so much a Stranger's ritual as a Native betrayal. In that, Kamakau's History suggested, the prophecy of the priest of Waimea, Kaopulupulu, was coming true. "White men would become rulers, the native population would live [landless] like fishes of the sea, the line of chiefs would come to an end, and a stubborn generation would cause the native race to dwindle."

Diachronic Flourishes

In 1799, six years after these events, the *Eliza*, a trader out of New Providence under Captain Gardiner, called at Waikiki. The first mate of the *Eliza*, a Welshman named Evans, had lived for some time on Oahu. He came to the captain's cabin and told Gardiner that the man who had killed Gooch and Hergest was in one of the canoes alongside. Gardiner went on deck with two muskets and the man jumped out of the canoe and began swimming away. The captain fired and missed. He then gave a pistol to an Hawaiian who went off in a canoe, shot the swimmer through the upper jaw and brought him back to the ship. They said that the man was an inferior chief, that he was black with tattoos, that his name was Koi. Captain Gardiner hanged him without ceremony.

Or was it Captain Brown of Providence who hanged him, not Captain Gardiner, or was it Captain Somebody Else? John Young, Kamehameha's beachcomber prime minister, told it differently for twenty-five years in the great cabins of ships that visited Hawaii. Or his listeners heard it differently. The details did not matter: the ironies did. But that, among other things, is History.

3

HISTORY IN THE MAKING

Discovery, Discipline, Discourse

It has been my prejudice of many years that the *Daedalus* was a messy ship. Long ago I had made what E. H. Carr had called an "historical fact" out of her visit to the Marquesas on her way to Hawaii. In the wild *mêlée* of excited curiosity on the beach that was the feature of early Marquesan-European encounters, a "young gentlemen" of the *Daedalus* was pinched, probed and had his hair pulled. This "rudeness" afforded the "Indians," wrote Vancouver, "as high an entertainment as it would have done an English rabble." The "poor fellow" "burst into a flood of tears!" Vancouver had made sense of wild native behavior by translating it into his own social class experience. The "young gentleman" had failed on two points. Then I did not know who the "young gentleman" was. Now I know it was William Gooch. Then I had pulled this rather unremarkable incident out of the ruck of many other unremarkable incidents to make a remark upon it, to make of it a parable about gestures that are not seen and words that are not heard in-between and within cultures. I had entered the significance of the event as an "historical fact" into an imaginary conversation that ethnohistorians were having about "culture-contact."

If historical facts are launched by historians with creative freedom, that license to make History is hedged about by two limitations–discipline and discovery. Historians are bound by the poetics of their particular kind of history, and the only past they can recover is the relics of it they find.

In discipline the poetics of making History are made explicit or, at least, historians are socialized reflectively to those poetics. Examination, grading, peer review, employment, promotion, tenure, publishing requirements are effective sanctions in the educating process to bend the historian's will to what proper history might be. They determine the limits of acceptability and distinguish disciplined history from a range of other histories–antiquarianism, journalism, romance, anecdote. They tune the disciplined historian's ear to hear the discourse. They make disciplined historians comfortable in their blinkered view.

In discourse the past is much more artifactual. Historical facts are much more shaped by the expedients of talk and the systems of understanding. None of us can plumb the depth of the plagiarism of our general discourse. Who can say what otherwise they might have been if Jesus Christ or Galileo or Marx or Freud had not spoken their sentences on life? None of us could measure precisely our own originality in our particular discourse any more than we can hear the difference between speech and language, *parole* and *langue*. That is the chief advantage of Otherness in time and space. Other different systems seem more observable in their differences. In our own time and space, the systems are blurred by our circumstantial experience. But every historian knows that someone will write his or her historiography–someone will observe my own Otherness. Someone will tell what I really said when I seemed to be saying something else. In this small ethnography where I am making History of making History, then, I can only suggest something of the discipline required. I can only suggest something of the discourse I self-consciously enter. I am present, expressed in my History, but I am more likely to see through the looking-glass than to see myself.

So let me begin again with my prejudice about the *Daedalus* to suggest how discipline and discourse drive me.

My historical fact of the "young gentleman" was a parable of the *Daedalus's* whole chaotic visit to the Marquesas. (This was preliminary to her reaching Waimea on the way from Cape Horn.) Hergest had made for the island of Tahuata and Cook's anchorage there. He missed it, however, and with difficulty beat back against the wind eventually to anchor at Vaitahu, or Resolution Bay. The Marquesans swarmed over the *Daedalus*, raucous and stealing. At 4:00 A.M., in a buffet of wind down the valley, the anchor cable broke. Then, as the *Daedalus* drifted towards the rocks of the shore, there was a cry of "fire." The crew had smelt smoke for days but only then found it came from the storagehold beneath the gunpowder room. The gunpowder room itself was stacked (against all navy rules) with badly stored goods. Damp bedding in the storagehold had self-combusted out of its own compost. They dared not open the fire to air, so they drilled a hole through the floor of the gunpowder room and poured water down. All was riot as part of the crew set sails, part dragged stores to the deck, part kept the Marquesans at bay. It would not have done for Captain Cook.

That was a beginning to my prejudice that the *Daedalus* was a messy ship. It was a prejudice reinforced by my inability to discover her papers. I could not discover them, despite looking in port records, in Admiralty papers, in the private papers of the Vancouver's expedition. My ignorance was a matter of some chagrin. With some pride for the pain endured, but with no evangelistic enthusiasm for it as historical method, I have a file, indeed an old fashioned file, of those cards that one dare not bend, spindle or staple, on every sailor who came into the Central Pacific in British and American naval vessels between 1767 and 1842, some ten thousand of them. I have known all the sailors on all the naval ships that have come to the central Pacific, save one. There has been one naval ship in the Pacific that has dashed my cliometric hopes. It has been the supply ship *Daedalus*.

Ships, especially naval ships, are not generally so elusive. It is a rare ship that in her making, in her manning, in all the ways that ships are touched by institutions of government and trade, does not leave some mark. The *Daedalus*, however, was in-between, part-navy, part-trade. Being hired, the *Daedalus* escaped the navy's institutional bonds. She had no naval archival accoutrement–the muster-rolls and logs–the lifeline of my cliometrics. The monthly muster-rolls registered the names of all aboard, their debts for tobacco and "slops," their fines of fifteen shillings for being found with the "venereals," what auction they had made for deadmen's clothes, what contribution they were docked for the chaplain, the credits of their monthly wage. The muster registered their demographic skeleton and their institutional portrait as well: their age, their place of origin, their ranks and promotions, whether they were pressed, whether they died, deserted or were discharged on the voyage. The logs, as many of them as there were commissioned officers and midshipmen, recorded the institutional events of every day–the orders given for sailing, the floggings, all things done under the Articles of War, the weather and navigation. There were no musters for the *Daedalus*, and Hergest's log has disappeared.

Of course, Richard Hergest, being naval, did not so easily escape. He had been able seaman aboard the *Adventure* on Cook's second voyage and midshipman aboard the *Resolution* on the third. He was thirty-seven years old when he commanded the *Daedalus*. Having spent more than twenty of those years in the navy, there was an imprint of Hergest's person already in navy records. In the awful days after Cook's death in Hawaii, when the crew of the *Resolution* had burned with hatred especially against a man they knew as "Britannee" whom they held responsible for Cook's killing, Hergest on one occasion had chased Britannee all the way to the Hawaiian lines. Hergest then snapped his pistol at close range, but it misfired. At Kauai when his commanding officer avoided another massacre by suffering the Hawaiian's "insolence," Hergest proclaimed that he would certainly have repressed the Hawaiians' insolence by force. He had not changed much in fourteen years. At Vaitahu in the Marquesas when William Gooch had burst into tears, Hergest had reproached him harshly for showing "so great a proof of his weakness"–weakness we might presume not just before natives but also before the non-gentlemen of the *Daedalus*. While Hergest berated Gooch, a Marquesan snatched a fowling piece from Hergest's hands. Impulsively Hergest ordered the mate to fire at the thief, but the mate's musket was not cocked. By that lucky accident the men escaped the consequences of Hergest's rashness, surrounded as they were by a large crowd. "To awe them into better behaviour," Hergest had musketoons fired over the Marquesans' heads. That did not create the required awe so he ordered a cannonade over their houses. In the end Hergest only got his fowling piece back when he kidnapped an obviously friendly "chief" and held him hostage.

Having confessed to a prejudice that the *Daedalus* was a messy ship as a beginning to my discourse on *why* it was a messy ship, having said I had not found the *Daedalus's* records, I have an embarrassing revelation to make. Let the embarrassment be my pledge to report what actually happens in making History. There *were* some official papers of the *Daedalus*, not musters and not strictly logs. I "found" them in the way historians find what has already been found some years before in the vast microfilm collection of the Australian Joint Copying Project. AJCP has microfilmed most of the public documentations of the Australian-Pacific past archived in the United Kingdom. These papers of the *Daedalus* were in a strange place. They were in the Board of Longitude collection. My embarrassment is that I did not ask myself why they were housed with the Board of Longitude or how that archiving would affect my reading. I did not read them at all properly.

I did not obey my own rule of discipline: that the texted past is contexted by its preservation. The papers were the workbooks of William Gooch, "Astronomer on board the Daedalus." There are two volumes, more than four-hundred pages of rough and untidy astronomical calculations. Gooch used these workbooks, in his term, to "fag" out his observations. At odd spots in the clutter of figures were notes to himself–rules for measuring the gain or loss of clocks, steps to be taken in measuring the angle of the moon. There were lists of Marquesan words and notes on the names of Marquesans he met. There were also some Latin and Greek phrases. *"Puella osculis dilectissima"* was one. "Delicious little girl with kisses" had been my translation. The Greek, I humbly confess, I did not translate, presuming they were quotes or transcriptions from some Greek classic. I did not see when I first scoured the microfilm two full pages of Greek script. Nor did I see, I also humbly confess, the list of the first names of most of the *Daedalus's* crew Gooch had jotted down to jog his memory and tucked away in the middle of his sums.

The Greek was not Greek at all. It was English in Greek letters. Gooch wrote it, I now know, as a sort of cipher. He would write drafts of letters in this script. Generally he wrote in this way for his father so that his mother and others would not understand the more exotic native customs he was describing. He and Richard Hergest also corresponded in this script. The two pages I first missed in his astronomical work book were a draft of a letter he wrote to Hergest while they were at Kealakekua Bay, Hawaii, just before they moved on to Waimea. It was a bitter and angry letter. Hergest's reproaches at Vaitahu had left deep wounds, and his reproaches at Kealakekua picked at their scabs.

Experiencing Inscriptions

The Past survives only in its relics, only in its inscriptions. Inscriptions are the expressions of what has happened. Inscriptions are written down or they are committed to a memory made social and public or they are caught in the shapes and forms of environments in buildings, in land-scapes, in artifacts. The Past when it survives is phrased in some message. It is also encoded in its symbolic forms.

Institutions at work inscribe lives in those dimensions of living that they touch–birth, death, tax, crime, membership. Storytellers, myth-makers, gossipers sculpt events with choice words and fine dramatics and pass them on by word of mouth so that their histories are embellished by each occasion of their telling, and in the end get caught by being written down. Participants in the events choose a genre–a diary, a letter, a poem, a newspaper–to clothe their interpretation of what has happened.

These relics of experience–always interpretation of the experience, never the experience itself–are all that there is of the Past. Historians never confront the Past, only the inscriptions that the Past has left. History is always interpretation of interpretation, always a reading of a given text.

Traditionally the word "sources" has been used to describe these inscriptions that mediate the past for historians. Sources are dubbed "primary" or "secondary." Historians know full well the ambivalence of calling something primary which is always after-the-event. Historians, nonetheless, would give some privilege to primary sources among these inscriptions. Primary sources are the inscriptions least intruded upon by interpretation and organization subsequent to the inscription's original making. Primary sources are as near the past experience as anything that has survived. Or they are counted by argument of the historian as being as near the past experience as anything that has survived. Labelling an inscription as a primary source gives it a character of authenticity and immediacy. It supports the conviction that the inscriptions are the Past itself.

"Sources" has the suggestion of originals, of fonts, of springs of real meaning. Primary sources become the mark of true history, become the mark of its realism. History is made real for schoolchildren by giving them archive kits so they can feel "as if" they confront the Past directly. Libraries, museums and archives hoard their primary sources: local historical societies are possessive of them: national prestige is measured in the millions of dollars that are paid for them. The urgency of preserving primary sources is always upon us. Memories, like cultures, are always about to be lost. The old, the eccentric, the powerful and now in more democratic days, Everyperson, is pursued relentlessly with a tape-recorder. In an era of limitless technological ambition there must be somebody planning the Giant Replay, an electronic Eternal *Nunc*.

Historians measure their own diligence by the miles of their trudging to see their primary sources. Using a primary source, something which is one of a kind, something in which there has been large social investment to collect and preserve, is a mark of privilege and status. Using primary sources means entering into silent contracts with individuals and institutions of varying freedom and trust. Access to them becomes a badge of status and familiarity. Status will determine whether a researcher handles an original document or only sees a microfilm of it. Using primary sources means absorbing their ambience of firstness and particularity. Finding them, understanding their relation to the institutions that preserve them, knowing how they lead to other primary sources is as much the historical act of interpretation as using them. Reading them is inseparable from the many different experiences of discovery–untying them, putting them in order, gingerly respecting their fragility, absorbing their many idiosyncracies, knowing the joy of surprise and the pain of long hours of finding nothing, or of nothing but contexting trivial detail. The realism of the Past in History is inseparable from the sense of realism gained from the search and the use of primary sources.

Let me say, not to seem immodest, nor indeed to rouse envy, but in the interests of a poetic of History, that this small project and pursuit of the *Daedalus* had taken me to the Mitchell Library (Sydney), the Alexander Turnbull Library (Wellington), the University of Hawaii Pacific Collection, the Hawaiian Children's Mission Library, the Bishop Museum, the State Archives (Honolulu), the Baker Library (Harvard), the University Library and various college collections (Cambridge), the British Library (London), the National Maritime Museum (Greenwich), the Norwich and Ipswich Public Record Offices. *Lloyd's Shipping Register* had showed that the *Daedalus* was 312 tons out of Whitby. She would have been (in my mind's image of her) pug-nosed and broad-beamed like Cook's *Endeavour*, also out of Whitby trade. Her owner when the Admiralty hired her in 1791 was an "A. Davison." He had bought her new just two years before, sheathed her with copper and put her on the London-St. Petersburg run.

On the day I had decided I was obliged–in the disciplinary interests of accuracy and exhaustiveness–to find out who "A. Davison" was, I happened to be in a local museum in King's Lynn, George Vancouver's birth place. I was innocently looking in a cabinet of Lord Horatio

Nelson mementos when I saw a medal for all the members of Nelson's victorious fleet in the battle of the Nile. The medal had been struck by one Alexander Davison. Alexander Davison was Nelson's agent. He retrieved the Admiral's prize money. He could easily afford the medal for the victory on the Nile.

Historians come to each relic of the Past, as geneticists come to double helixes, without context, out-of-order. It is in the prefaces of their books and in rationalizing hindsight that they see the order of their understanding.

Narrating Structures

I had begun to look for Mr. Davison because I sensed that the messiness of the *Daedalus* was not so much circumstantial as structural, that Hergest's problems were as much in role as in personality. My discourse is about ships. I write ethnographies of ships in the special circumstances of their meetings with the Other. I puzzle at the sort of cultural systems Stranger's ships displayed to Native islands. In the 15th century, Europeans discovered the inhabited earth was all islands in one great ocean. The whole world became Native to the European Stranger. I had a thesis that Native and Stranger were environmental to one another, were in a symbiotic relationship. One cannot make History of this bound-together reality without describing the public systems of signs of each, separate and together. I would do the culture history of Strangers in their ships, of Natives in their islands, of their possession of one another.

When the *Daedalus* finally reached Nootka Sound after the tragedy at Waimea, Vancouver found most of the supplies she brought were bad, ruined or useless. It might have reminded Vancouver that the realities of empire were not in ceremonies of possession, but in the many links in the chain of hegemony of the likes of Mr. Davison. For that greedy merchant, empire and voyages of discovery were sacred cows for the milking.

The Admiralty had ordered Vancouver to send the *Daedalus* from Nootka Sound to Botany Bay on the southeast coast of Australia. Vancouver had stalls fitted on the *Daedalus* and loaded her with twelve cows, six bulls and eighteen sheep to supply the penal settlement. If we were making History in another cause or discourse, this action of Vancouver would not pass without comment. 1988 is the bicentenary of the settlement of Botany Bay and *much* History is being made. The *realpolitik* of empires is often nothing more than a world made manageable by lines on a map. A line that joined Nootka Sound and Botany Bay made a satisfying vision of global strategy. A navy that needed to lose its dependence on Russia for its timber might make a sphere of influence of northwest forests and cheap convict labor at Botany Bay. There was more. Vancouver was ordered to send the *Daedalus* to Botany Bay by way of New Zealand. At New Zealand she was to pick up two Maoris to take to Botany Bay to instruct the convicts on dressing flax, to make sails for ships no less.

Lieutenant James Hanson, who replaced the dead Hergest, was ordered to proceed to the Marquesas and Tahiti before going to New Zealand. Hergest had died thinking he had discovered (and Gooch had mapped) the northern group of the Marquesas. But a Frenchman, Etienne Marchand, and two Americans, Joseph Ingraham and Josiah Roberts, had beaten them by a few months and had put their separate revolutions on the Pacific map. Hanson, by Vancouver's orders, was also to rescue some shipwrecked seamen from Tahiti. This was another imperializing gesture, making lines of communication safe.

Only fifteen of the thirty crew of the *Daedalus* were well enough to work the ship when they arrived at Nukuhiva in the Marquesas. There is still no log extant to record this second chaotic visit. But a poetic, if rheumatic, bo'sun called William House wrote some lines:

There's no keeping these natives from thieving and plunder.
Without muskets and guns to make lightning and thunder.

Mistaking canoes that were returning from their own local war as attacking the ship, the *Daedalus* ran out of Taiohae Bay, all guns and muskets blazing.

At Tahiti two of the crew deserted. One of them, Peter Haggerstein, a Swede, was to have an important impact on Tahitian politics and the London Mission Society's future evangelizing efforts. Add one name to my collection of the *Daedalus's* crew. Add one sentence to my discourse on Native and Stranger and the beachcombers who mediated cultures.

Hanson took the *Daedalus* to Doubtless Bay, New Zealand. Without anchoring, he enticed two Maoris out of their canoes on board and made off with what he could only hope were flax dressers. At Port Jackson, Governor Arthur Phillip ruefully remarked to his superiors that none of the livestock from Nootka survived, that the two Maoris had about one hour of information on flax between them.

In this first part of the *Daedalus's* voyage, the crew had survived fire and shipwreck in the Marquesas, three had been killed at Waimea, three had deserted at Nootka, they had blasted their way out of Nukuhiva, two more had deserted in Tahiti, they had kidnapped two Maoris in New Zealand. Most of the supplies the *Daedalus* had brought to Vancouver were rotten and damaged. All the supplies she had brought to Port Jackson had perished. My prejudice that she was a messy ship stands. She did, however, sail home to England with sails made of flax by convicts.

Norbert Elias, with his constant interest at the expression of social structures in everyday symbolic forms, once began a study of British naval vessels of the 16th and 17th centuries. It was a study he seems not to have completed. In his view an early naval vessel held within it a structural contradiction. It was a ship of war. It had a double function, to sail and to fight. In its capacity to sail, a ship was serviced by seamen who had learned their craft by many years of application. They were governed by a master who was legitimated to authority out of his knowledge and expert skills. In its capacity to fight, a ship was serviced by captains and lieutenants with their soldiers (become marines). Captains had been squires and knights. They came with their own bonded men. They came with the king's commission. Captains were gentlemen born to authority. They were insiders to power legitimized and established with infinite ceremony but outsiders to the running of the ship.

Let me complete for the *Daedalus* what Norbert Elias had begun. The structures of naval vessels were supported and the tensions created by their contradictions were eased only by extraordinary effort. Naval ships were artificial, distorted segments of life. Large numbers of men were dependent on one another for safety and comfort, and that dependence was built on a relationship that was neither familial nor servile. It was a totally public life with no privacy, but it was filled with boundaries none the less. Boundaries divided quarter-deck and lower-deck and made distinctions of status and function from boy to commander, between messes, divisions, watches and masts. Daily life was full of physical gestures that marked position and privilege, that established group existence, that drew and redrew boundaries according to the needs of maintaining the ship. Life was full of conflict that boundary-drawing engendered and full of rituals of conflict resolution either imposed from on high in discipline and punishment or resolved from below in fights and deference to ceremony. Power and authority were constantly reified in such public ceremonies as the scrutinized measurement of every bodily need, or in the display of the king's delegated commission in the reading of the Articles of War, or in the reversed world of "skylarking" on deck and the rituals of crossing the equator. In the total institution of a naval ship persons were owed little. Role and rule were owed everything. But there was exchange as well. Deviance from order was the principal crime, but encroachment on the rights that were held behind these boundaries was the principal injustice.

Hence the ambivalence of the *Daedalus*: Hergest, with twenty-two years of socialization in being a navy commander, found himself commanding, but with none of the customary ritual and symbolic supports. Where gestures of distance and depersonalization on a navy

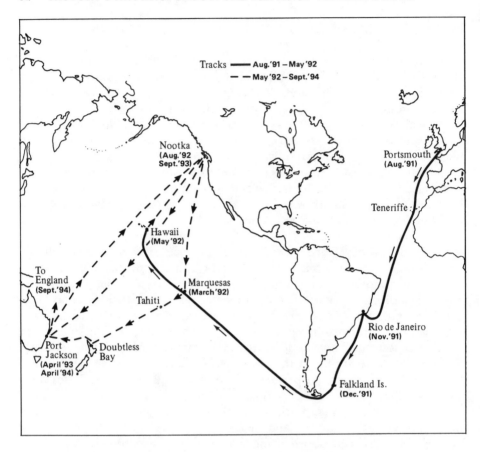

FIGURE 4: THE VOYAGE OF THE *DAEDALUS*, 1791-1794.

vessel would have given his authority power, on the *Daedalus* his captaincy was mediated by mates and masters who belonged to the crew more than the crown. At Teneriffe in the Atlantic, the *Daedalus's* first stop, the crew had become riotously drunk. The Spaniards at Teneriffe, because of this, refused them water. Hergest had gone to the forecastle and had tried to manhandle a drunken Irishman into his hammock. At this moment another drunk attempted to "collar" Hergest. Next morning the Irishman challenged Hergest's right to "break his neck" and declared he would take no more orders. He deserted at Rio de Janeiro with two others. Hergest had to live with what in every other circumstance of naval life would have been a mutinous crew. Men were sometimes hanged for striking an officer; they were always flogged. At Rio the deserters were simply replaced by three Portuguese. One of them was Manuel.

The *Daedalus* was disturbed by other contradictions created by Mr. Davison. William Gooch, I now know, did not like Mr. Davison. "A dirty rascal," he called him. Hergest concurred: "Mr. G., that Davison is a merchant and merchants are such damned strange sets of animals as perhaps you've never dealt with...!" As it happened, Gooch was not far wrong. Davison was on the verge of becoming an intimate to the great, a friend of princes and possessed of an immense fortune. England was developing large barracks of troops as she waited for Napoleon's invasion. In 1795 the commission to supply those barracks with furniture, bedding, candles and coal was taken away from local suppliers and given in virtual monopoly to Davison at $2\frac{1}{2}\%$ commission for everything he supplied. Davison discovered that if he retailed those goods himself he could get good prices as well as his $2\frac{1}{2}\%$ commission. He then discovered that if he could collect the army's payment before the commissariate received his goods the millions of pounds would capitalize his industries. He quickly became a very wealthy man, later brought low, it has to be said, by the retirement of the general who gave him the commission and by the discovery by a Parliamentary Committee of the general's somewhat evasive accounts. The committee was not amused at coal with 30% water content being sold by Davison at ninety shillings a load at 40% retail profit and $2\frac{1}{2}\%$ commission. Mr. Davison was a very dirty rascal.

He hired the *Daedalus* to the navy. He provided all the supplies she carried. He clearly planned as well to have her trade on the northwest coast and in the Pacific. She was to make a little money on the side in otter skins and curios. The *Daedalus's* distracted state when she anchored at Waimea came from her divided nature.

The crew of the *Daedalus* were not just divided and ambivalent to themselves. They were ambivalent and divided to the Hawaiians as well. The Hawaiians were adept at reading the signs of flags and meeting the representatives of kings. They mimicked or translated empire in their civilizing process. Since Cook's death all their attacks had been on traders. They had not much chance to see, as Vancouver afterwards tried to teach them, that the *Daedalus* was different. If Hergest was in uniform, the others on the *Daedalus* certainly were not. There were no signs of captaincy, no disciplined exchange. Being a naval agent, on the margins of both navy and trade was the death of Richard Hergest, and with him William Gooch.

Recurrent Findings

I am ahead of myself with my story of Hergest at Teneriffe and my quotations of William Gooch. I was making sense of the *Daedalus* as a ship of ambiguities. Those ambiguities rose out of Hergest's personal imprudence and rashness, certainly, but more out of his inability to impose order ceremonially, to establish the sacred space of the quarter-deck, the social distance of a commander, the territoriality of his role. There were as well the ambiguities of empire that Vancouver displayed–the extended power that was present but not resident. There were the ambiguities in empire that Davison displayed–the rhetoric of civilized propriety and the reality of venal interest. Those ambiguities were my narrative, my history, of the *Daedalus*.

I was once reflecting on these ambiguities in a series of lectures on "Native and Stranger" at the University of Hawaii, when I discovered that William Gooch was a Cambridge man. Marshall Sahlins told me. Cambridge men are too valuable to miss the net of history. There is a register of nearly every Cambridge man that ever was, *Alumni Cantabrigienses*.

> Gooch, William; son of William Gooch, of Brockdish, Norf. Born there. School, Stradbroke (private), two years, under Mr. Mack. Age 16. Admitted sizar, May 30 1786.

> B.A. 1791 (2nd wrangler). Scholar, Michs 1786 to L. Day 1791. Junior fellow L. Day 1791 to his death. Smith's prize, 1791. Schuldham college prize, 1791. He was the son of a poor village haircutter; sent to college by the liberality of Sir Thomas Hesilrige, and other neighbours. He went out as astronomer, on a voyage of discovery in the Pacific. Murdered, together with a lieutenant of the ship, by the natives, at Woahoo, near Hawaii, May 13 1792 (Europ. Mag. xxiii.319; Chr. Rememb.I.19). There are a number of letters in the University Library (Mm6.48): for extracts, see C. Wordsworth's Scholae Acad., p. 319.

"There are a number of letters in the University Library!" His relics are his bundle of papers: letters of thanks to the sponsors who sent him, a poor boy, to Cambridge University; letters written in excitement at the door of the examination hall on the threshold of his triumph as a student; letters written in the antechamber of the Board of Longitude as the Board decided on his future and he begins to be caught in the politics of patrons; letters describing his entry into the world of science and of ships; then long letter-journals of his voyage in the *Daedalus* to Teneriffe, to Rio de Janeiro, to the Falklands, the Marquesas and finally to

Hawaii. They are an extraordinary collection, so innocent, so intimately revealing that it seems prurient to read them, as he educates his parents to the complexities of his new status, as he displays his inner self in his new environment to "Goody Two-Shoes" the young lady he affianced in the last days before leaving England in the *Daedalus*.

There is the irony. The *Daedalus*, bereft of its public person in the expected naval records, is known through a private experience, written down more personally than on any ship I have known.

The distance between Brockdish, in the county of Norfolk, and the University of Cambridge, in the neighboring county, was not great. But distance, like time, is much social as physical, and for a poor boy, son of a barber, the halls of Gonville and Caius College were a long way from his father's cottage and his village school. So William Gooch's letters home to his parents in November 1790 as he prepared for his public disputations in the university Schools, and in January 1791 as he sat for his examinations in the Senate Hall of the university were full of quiet pride as he described how well he had done to be Second Wrangler, and how near he had come to being the most honored student of the university. He educated his parents to the customs and lore of his new life, quieted his mother's fears for the effects of vigorous exertion on his health, gossiped with his father about his new network of friends a little below the gentry. He was engaging, simple and discreet. It would be the small triumph of his short twenty-two years of life that he was a comfortable stranger in spaces not quite his own. It would be his life's irony that he died a stranger in spaces he could never own.

Young William Gooch's letters now lie nearly two-hundred years later in the library of his university. You will need proper credentials to read them, some testimony from your academic institution that you are a *bona fide* scholar. You will need to sign some declaration making it clear you know who really owns this part of the past. The special room with its special hours, the idiosyncracies of the officials who husband the documents, the sounds in silence will context your reading of the letters, like the memory of a writer's voice in the words of a printed page. The past become cultural artifact accrues much in its history making. For its poetics you will need your practiced scholarly poses. There are the territorial signals you will make and observe as you mark the boundaries of your library seat with disarray or tidiness. There is your nonchalance or furious busyness as you wait delivery of your bundled part of the past. There are your deferences to its owners. There is the brazenness of your eye contact as you enter and learn who sits where: Do you always sit in the same place? Yes, you do. Why do you do it? Long ago you will have acquired a medley of defenses against the loud voices of unpracticed inquirers; perhaps you have even conquered your fear of the pencil sharpener that is loudly disturbing. You have learned to balance servility and professional dignity in your deferences to the possessive and disdainful among the librarians. The past you uncover will never be separated from the occasion and the mode of your discovering it. Perhaps it will not be a different past for that, but it will be your own, and your creations will be more confident for the reality of your experience. You will join the past dispersed in different places with the commonality of your experience. You will collapse the times and the spaces of the past into the unity of your own perceiving.

William Gooch's papers (now manuscript Mm6.48 in the Cambridge University library) make a sad bundle. They were collected by his father as a reliquary of his son's life and left by the father at his own death to a Mr. C. Doughty, tanner, a worthy of Brockdish village, long-time friend and then executor of old William Gooch's will. Mr. Doughty, the tanner, no doubt with a sense of reverence for a history that was larger than himself or feeling some obligation to give resurrection to the promise of young William Gooch, gave the letters to the most famous topographer or local historian in the county, David Turner. David Turner shaped them a little more by adding a recollection of a schoolmate of William Gooch, a few notes in the hand of the famous Sir Joseph Banks, and a letter of a young Thomas Dobson to his father, a wine merchant near Vauxhall. Thomas Dobson had been a witness to Gooch's death. No doubt, too, David Turner, local antiquarian and in some competition with other local historians, had a collector's possessiveness for history. What had first been a reliquary of a father's love and pride, and then an executor's obligation to posterity, became a thing of historical beauty, displaying the triumphs of Turner's searches and the happy accidents of his findings.

Turner gave his collection–and who will say there is less joy in public giving than there is in public collecting?–to the University of Cambridge. In his letter of donation that doubles as a prefatory note to these "Letters Memoranda and Journal containing the History of Mr. Gooch," he remarked: "Whatever is now known or can hence forward be known of William Gooch is contained in this volume which consists of original documents respecting him and in his own hand-writing." "William Gooch was an only child," he adds. "A dutiful, affectionate child, so raised above his original station and so full of hope itself and so calculated to excite it in others, is taken from his parents in a humble sphere of life and so dashed to the ground their present joy and future comfort and glory." The curious wonder of it all for the university, he suggested, was that from the same small village school of Harleston, near Brockdish, and from the same schoolmasters, Mr. Henry Tilney and Mr. Mack, came Professor Samuel Vince, Plumerian Professor of Mathematics at Cambridge, the Reverend John Brinkley, Astronomer Royal in Dublin and Bishop of Cloynes, and William Gooch, Second Wrangler of 1791.

Before and After in a Present

It is not true, as David Turner suggested, that all we know of William Gooch is contained in the volume of his papers. Nor is it true, that he was an only child. It is a rare human being that does not leave some mark of his or her institutional person just by being born or dying, being taxed or counted, being political, being religious, being the object of welfare or law. The people of Brockdish made their delible and indelible marks in parish registers and in the stone of their church and its graveyard. Their principal register was of baptisms and deaths but in the second half of the 18th century they had to tax themselves to support their deserving poor, and twice yearly, come Easter and Lady's Day, the reckoning of their taxes and the accounting of its expenditure was the responsibility of the Overseers of the Poor.

The register of baptisms and deaths at Brockdish is a small book of vellum. Depending on how one holds it in the hand, the register begins in 1757 with baptisms, or, turned upside down, with deaths. Probably only a clerical economy but also some sign of theological ambivalence as to where the Book of Life really begins.

The register is an untidy one with more than a suggestion that many an entry is an afterthought. The village at Brockdish was small and of no great social significance. The priest, as often as not, resided more comfortably elsewhere. Perhaps young William Gooch was baptized on an absent-minded day. Squeezed in along the margin is the notation: "William the son of William and Sarah Gooch was born April 3, baptized May 8th 1770." There is as well a crabbed entry all awry: "Mary, daughter of William and Sarah Gooch, May 8 1774." And elsewhere, "Sarah, d of William and Sarah Gooch. Born Aug 1767." Perhaps in becoming churchwarden, old William Gooch took the opportunity to make his own children's history, where others had been more careless. There is less mystery about Sarah than about Mary. Sarah's death at the age of ten years is registered in the same vellum book on 23 March 1777, and amongst the Overseers accounts is the bill of a Dr. Henry Brabant who came on visits to Brockdish in February and March 1777, giving "an opinion in the smallpox." William and Sarah Gooch lost their eldest child Sarah in that epidemic. It killed sixteen others of the village as well. Perhaps Mrs. Gooch, who was thirty-two years old when Sarah was born and thirty-five when William was born, at thirty-nine lost the infant Mary and no one registered so inconsequential a death. Certainly the fear of losing their son after Sarah's death troubled them. They then lived long lives in the shadow of their realized fears. Sarah and mother and father lie side by side as close to the southern wall of the Brockdish church as they could be. Son William's bones had a more disturbing and disturbed burial.

Brockdish lies on the rolling downs where Norfolk becomes Suffolk, its church on a hill, its houses in the valley along the Waveney River. Brockdish (*broc dic*) means 'broad ditch' and that has suggested to some that the river Waveney was once a stronger waterway than it has ever been in the memories of hundreds of years. But the ghosts of Saxons and Danes are pale, and it is difficult to imagine that the river played any great part in Brockdish's establishment and continuity. Brockdish is not really on the crossroads to anywhere. Norwich is only fourteen miles to the north, but the Brockdish road beside the Waveney leads to Yarmouth to the northeast and branches southwest to different destinations on the flatlands and in the fens. The road southwest went easily by Bury St. Edmunds, past Newmarket and Stourbridge Fair, against whose dissipations preachers warned Cambridge students even in the 18th century.

At Brockdish, the grey stone Church of St. Peter's and Paul's stands on a hill to the west of the village, set with its rectory apart from the houses in the valley. There were forty-three rateable households in the freehold parish in 1786, and the population was somewhere near 350. From before Domesday, abbeys and bishoprics, earls and dukes had owned the land around the village in two large parcels. In the years of our interest, the social focus of the village and the reason for its livelihood was the Manor and the Hall. Both had been owned by a succession of gentry families in the 18th century with no great stability. In 1786 the Hall belonged to Thomas Maynard, a Cambridge University man of Emmanuel College but then thirty years away from his schools.

William Gooch's father was variously described as village barber, haircutter and peruke- or wig-maker. Perhaps there was a history of his social advance in these descriptions. More likely, to an outsider's view, there was little social distinction between them. He himself, under the influence of the lawyer who helped him make his will, called himself "peruke-maker." It is difficult to imagine what fortunes there were to be made in either peruke-making or barbering in a village of 350 souls, but in an age in which cosmetic attention to hair was strong, daily coiffure and powdering by one's barber was a common requirement of gentlemen and ladies even in so unmetropolitan a society as Brockdish. William Gooch's visits to the Manor and Hall would have been frequent and, if fortunes were not to be made nor social boundaries to be crossed, the daily visit of the peruke-maker was a between-classes liaison of confidences and information. The talents of the barber's son came naturally to be known to those whose greater fortunes could help him. In any case, Thomas Maynard, later the baronet Sir Thomas Maynard Hesilrige, seems to have provided young William Gooch's opportunity to go to Cambridge. But networks and upward social mobility are more complicated than that.

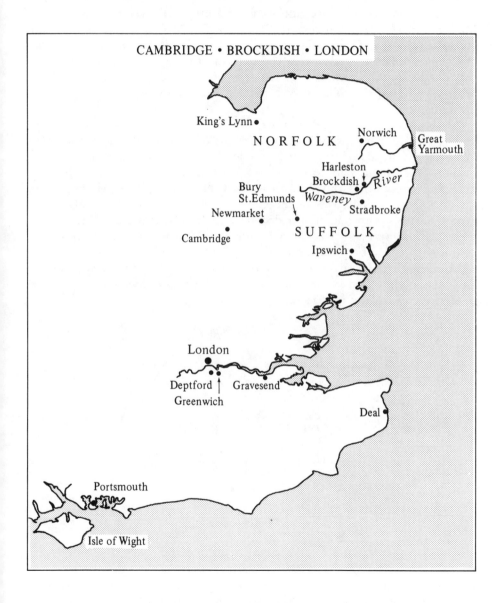

FIGURE 5: EAST ANGLIA.

William and Sarah Gooch lived more than fifty years in Brockdish. From 1773 until 1817, when they died, they lived in the same house, invariably rated at £4 and paying twice yearly levies that ranged between three and nine shillings. There were eleven houses in the village valued less than theirs, twenty-six houses valued more and six the same. The Manor and the Hall, valued at £126 and £105 respectively, and seven cottages valued at £2 was the range of valuation. So by public estimation William and Sarah lived nearer the bottom of the scale of living than the top or the middle. All their lives their house was designated as "Mr. Webster's." Half the village were tenants like themselves, but also just as permanent.

At the beginning of the extant Overseer's Records in 1773 and 1774, and therefore perhaps before that, William Gooch was rated for "Mr. Webster's" and also for a "Dr Schouldham's" house, valued at £5. Dr. Francis Schuldham had connections with Cambridge University. Indeed he was a fellow of Gonville and Caius College and is described in the history of the college as a member of a "thorough Norfolk family" with a coat of arms who had sent a dozen of their sons to Caius. The doctor died in 1776, and the "late Dr Schouldham's" house was rented to others in the village. He bequeathed a gift to his college of an annual prize of a piece of plate to be given to the most deserving scholar. Young William Gooch won the prize in 1791 and in his papers, in a shakey hand not his own, is a copy of the inscription:

In Scholis Philosophicis

Optime inter suos Caienses respondenti

DD

Franciscus Schuldham MD

Collegii Gonv et Caius Socius

Praemium Meruit

Guielmus Gooch

A.D. 1791

Perhaps William Gooch's father used the house belonging to Dr. Schuldham for a work place; perhaps, being a barber, he was his medical assistant.

We have to think that both village and parents enjoyed the triumph and the double connection with Cambridge University. There are many village names that appeared in young William Gooch's letters–spinsters, innkeepers, tradesmen, who supported him with gifts of food and clothes or with gifts to be given away such as a hare for the Fellows' table. There were other villagers too poor to be rated and beneficiaries of the overseer's welfare, who derived more vicarious joy by inquiring for his health and sending supportive messages. Young William often felt guilty for his tardiness as a correspondent. Nonetheless he joined them all to him with news meant to be conveyed by his father.

Dr. Schuldham's residence was only one sign among many pointing Brockdish in East Anglia toward Cambridge University. There were many livings in the area at the distribution of Gonville and Caius College. Each of the colleges at the university looked for students among different classes and regions. Gonville and Caius depended for many years on East Anglia and gave preference in their bursaries to the poorer scholars from the lowland counties. It is possible that it was William Gooch's boyhood ambition to become a priest, and, if so, a presumption that he would become one through Gonville and Caius College. His father, if he was an instrument of fashion at Brockdish, was also an ecclesial person. Briefly old William Gooch was constable of the village and then, for most of his fifty years at Brockdish, churchwarden. Churchwardens at the time were likely to come from the social order of skilled artisans and tradesmen. They needed only moderate respectability to take responsibility for the church's physical welfare and social conscience. They did not always need to be pious. But old William Gooch by all accounts was both respectable and pious. When he died in 1817 his parish priest, Samuel Reeve (a Gonville and Caius man) squeezed a short judgement beside a notation of his death in the brand new parish register of deaths and burials. The chancy vellum volume had gone, and the essentials of life and death were now, by law of George IV, recorded coldly and uniformly in ruled columns. But Reeve made a small testimony of his edification from having known William Gooch: "*Vir eximius, pius, et benevolus, virtutibus omnibus bono, vitae longissimae enituit.*"

The Reverend Reeve also took the trouble to write a letter to the *Christian Remembrancer,* forwarding a bequest of William Gooch of £5. One can see in the letter that lives can be exemplary for all sorts of reasons. Reeve, as a priest of the established church, took a dim view of methodistic prophets and their "spirit of fanaticism." Old William Gooch, on the contrary, was exemplary of old-fashioned virtue–not quite extinct in village life, the editor added. One can see as well that the death of the son had already become inextricable from the life of the father. And, as in all parables about the past, significance was more important than accuracy. So, as the priest's letter told the story of the boy's death, it did not matter that he confused the Hawaiian Islands with the Friendly (or Tongan) Islands. They were both equidistant from civilization. And it seemed natural to Reeve that an astronomer would go ashore in the line of his duty to make observations. What William Gooch was actually doing when he died was less important than what he should have been doing. The Past is so malleable to presumption.

There are clear signs that the father was exemplary to his son as well as to the institutional church. They are to be seen in the son's gentle sensitivity and the balance of his self-depreciation and confidence. Young William Gooch's move to Cambridge was less a calling to the priesthood than a presumption that he would follow the natural direction of his education. There were no signs of spiritual trauma or of sudden discovery or of guilty depression. His depressions were not religious. They concerned his laziness in doing his work, his guilt in not fulfilling social obligations and promises. He noted the marriages and the ordinations of his friends at college as choices that closed the option of becoming a scholar (celibacy was a requirement of university fellows) and choices that coupled freedom with security. He never wrote directly of himself and the priesthood. The opportunity to go to the Pacific as an astronomer crowded in too quickly to allow more long-term reflection. He told a story, however, showing that others thought the priesthood and higher honors were inevitable for him. In the last days before going to the Pacific, he was making his farewells to a Mrs. Fearon, the mother of one of his Cambridge friends. "She used to tell me when I came back and was made a bishop I should preach at Ely Place Chapel and she would walk back with me and amaze her neighbours with her grand visitor. She put on a cheerful countenance and told me three years hence she would be getting the lawn sleeves ready and burst into tears as she finished."

When he did leave, he took with him a number of pious books and placed them in his cabin: the Bible, of course, in English and Greek, the *Common Prayer Book* in English and Greek, Bishop Sherlocks's *Sermons* and Robert Nelson's *The Practice of True Devotion, in Relation to the End as well as the Means of Religion, with an Office for Holy Communion.* Robert Nelson's *True Devotion* described a piety near what one imagines the ideal of William Gooch to have been. It decried putting trust and devotion into the "means" of religion–prayer, hearing the word of God, sacraments, meditation and examination. It proposed, instead, a discipline of everyday life. Being rightly motivated and blessed with reflection, being careful for moderation of every sort, being rational and directed was a practice of Christianity, not just a "form of godliness." It was a formula, of which there were many, for being in the world but not of it, of being religious but not at a distance from both in the separated religion of monastery or "fanaticism." In the young astronomer, as we shall see, this pragmatism, this modernism, had other expressions. He mediated–to use a Sartrean term–a changing cultural understanding of the relationships between knowing, believing, and being. He was exemplar to himself of changes more widely experienced.

The last will and testament of Gooch's father is a textual expression of this mediation. Small things have large significance. It is perhaps somewhat surprising that a peruke-maker from a small village would make a last will and testament, but William Gooch as churchwarden had spent a great deal of his life accounting for things. Also, with the death of his son and with no natural heir, he had to make a bequest, had to reify his life in the things he distributed. He had, in fact, in his world turned upside-down to bequeath what his son had bequeathed him.

Half the letters in Mm6.48 in the Cambridge University Library are the correspondence between William Gooch's father and Dr. Nevil Maskelyne, the Astronomer Royal who as Secretary to the Board of Longitude, administered young William Gooch's employment and was his legal executor. Maskelyne, with great care for proprieties and considerable sensitivity to the old man's sorrow and bewilderment, calculated and negotiated for what was left in pounds, shillings and pence of the dead boy's life. So it had to be decided whether the boy died on 13 May 1792 by the naval calendar or 12 May by the civil calendar. It made the difference of the day's pay owed. It also had to be decided whether, when "dead men's clothes" were auctioned on a ship on which the captain was purser, the captain's secretary got the purser's commission. (Captain Bligh, just back from his mutiny, was consulted, and said he had his doubts). And what were the lawyers' and naval agents' proper fees? Gooch's father had to auction off his son's books. Of what use were Homer, Virgil, Demosthenes, Locke's *On Human Understanding*, Whiston's *Euclid*, Parkinson's *Mechanics* now? They sold for £10/14/0, less duty and commission, at the White Bear Inn, Cambridge. And there was a last gift to be made, Newton's *Principia*. His son's tutor, Richard Belward, was given the book as a sign of gratitude for "the singular friendship and respect the college has shewed to my dear son during his whole time there from his first admission." The college itself found remnants of a benefit owed. When Nevil Maskelyne made his final accounting, he had £149/14/8 to send to the father. When all was calculated, William and Sarah Gooch received £176/1/5 for the life of their son.

Sarah Gooch died on 21 April 1817 in her eighty-second year. After a lifetime of mourning for a son, William Gooch had no heart for a long bereavement for his wife. He made his will by July and was dead by November. His fortune from his son's estate had grown a little to £215. He made of it many gifts. His will was a map of the extensions of his life and a history of memorable occasions and caring relationships, irretrievable to us, known in the reception of his giving. His public charities came first: £10 to the Bible Society, £10 to the Church Missionary Society, £5 for the London Society for the Conversion of the Jews, £5 for the Society for the Promoting of Christian Knowledge. Being Church, William Gooch knew the world and touched its systems. His most private charity came next and he was most careful to organize its continuity. There was £15 out of which his executors were to pay "Thomas Denny, then residing in Kendenhall with the Harleston workhouse, sixpence a week during his natural life, the first payment to commence the Monday next after my decease." Thomas Denny was too poor to wait on lawyer's colder proprieties. He was "at need," as the Overseer's accounts would put it, when sixpence or a shilling served the poor better than a blanket or a half chauldron of coal or an old pair of breeches, or nursing them or burying them. Thomas Denny was one of those whose house in 1786 had been valued at £10 and who had paid a tax twice as much as William Gooch had ever paid. The Misses Denny, sisters or daughters, sent small gifts to young William at Cambridge. Their bad financial times got registered in the Overseers' books with all the rest. Indeed, as William Gooch parcelled his fortune into £5 and £10 lots, one can see his charity directed not just to a poor deserving by reason of their bond to him but directed to those in some alliance with him in the business of serving the poor. In the economy of the poor in the small world of Brockdish there was a give in charity and a take in trade. If the Dewmilk's child needed burying then John Jeffries got a shilling and sixpence for digging the grave and tolling the bell. If coal was needed, then someone was paid nine shillings to cart it and someone else twopence to unload it. Generally Mr. Mann provided the coal. "To my good friend William Mann of London, gentleman, £10 to purchase such a piece of plate as he shall think proper as a present to his eldest daughter." Gooch's connections were much wider than Brockdish, but they were regional nonetheless. His bequests went mostly south to the Suffolk villages of Spexhall, Ilketshale, Wesleton, Syleham, Weybread, but also, in nearby Norfolk, to Redenshall, Harleston, Kendenhall. They went to family members of whom there is no other mention in his life— the children of his late brother Matthew and his widow Hannah Gooch. They went to farmers, husbandmen, gentlemen and, of course, the tanner, C. Doughty. They were carefully directed to the children of these friends but entrusted to their parents. And, careful man that he was in all the public responsibilities of his life, he transferred the obligations he had as others' legal executor to someone else. He must have felt, as he prepared to die, that his life had come to a very tidy end.

His son, who had been a somewhat less organized person, was equally attentive to the small proprieties of Christian living. He was as ecclesial as his father, and if the Reverend Samuel Reeve and the editor of the *Christian Remembrancer* had known him as they thought they knew his father, they would have recognized the same practical piety. Young William Gooch did not declare his spiritual calling to the priesthood nor did he declare a venal interest in it. He was like his father. A certain venal interest was inextricably present in the structures that bound their lives. Who could say that they themselves did not profit by their own charity or by their own idealism? They seemed to balance, however, their self-interest and the interests of others more nicely than most.

William and Sarah Gooch, living in Mr. Webster's house in Brockdish and always possessive of their remaining child William, had scarcely trusted the carefulness of others for their son. Charitable in all respects, they were reluctant givers of their boy. Sarah Gooch is a silent figure to us; we would not even know her name except for the register of baptisms and deaths. She was off-stage in young William Gooch's small dramas. He quieted her worries about his riding in wet clothes, he explained his needs for life in the tropics, above all, he begged her agreement to his plans. But, all indirectly, he heard of her, and sent messages to her, through his father.

A Mr. C. Nicholl, alderman and Justice of the Peace at Yarmouth, wrote to David Turner, the antiquarian collector, nearly fifty years after these events that "being an only child [William Gooch] was the object of the most tender solicitude to both father and mother who seldom permitted him to mix with other children except in their presence. How far this seclusion might operate in forming studious habits, it is impossible to say, but it is certain that, at school, his timidity deterred him from participating in schoolboy sports and drove him to seek amusement in reading." There being no school at Brockdish, his parents had to let him go as far as Harleston, three or four miles along the road to Yarmouth. And they may have let him go to Stradbroke about the same distance across the river into Suffolk.

The reason for being hesitant about his Stradbroke schooling is that while the same Mr. Nicholl said he was a "chum" of William for six or seven years at Harleston, J.V. Venn, the writer of the definitive biographical history of *Alumni Cantabrigienses* says of Gooch: "son of William Gooch, of Brockdish, Norf. Born there. School, Stradbroke (private), two years under Mr. Mack."

At Harleston in 1688, William Sandcroft, Archbishop of Canterbury, settled £54 per annum on the master, fellows and scholars of Emmanuel College, Cambridge, to nominate a chaplain and a schoolmaster on condition that they hold "a publick school for the education of youth in some convenient place." They were to give them a "common ground of learning in the excellent catechism of the Church of England and cause them to get perfectly by hearing the Nicene and Athanasian Creeds, the

Te Deum, and prayers of the primmer and common prayerbook fit for any good Christian to learn and use, and to take care that the scholars were constantly present at the prayer of the church and that they behave themselves soberly and piously there, and be taught such gestures and made such answers as the church subscribes." The school-master in the 1770's was Henry Tilney, and several sources are agreed that he taught not only William Gooch but two other notable scholars, Professor Vince and Bishop Brinkley. Probably, William Gooch was educated by Tilney at Harleston in his early years and in the final two years of his schooling, aged fourteen and fifteen, he went to Stradbroke. There are no records in public places of either the school at Stradbroke or Mr. Mack. But in his letters, Gooch sent respectful messages both to Mr. Tilney and Mr. Mack and had qualms of conscience that he never fulfilled his obligation of keeping Mr. Mack informed on his progress in mathematics and astronomy.

Stradbroke at the end of the 18th century was poorer than Brockdish. All of Suffolk was suffering with the decline of the knitting industries and the consequent rise in the migrant and resident poor. It was no time for flourishing public education in East Anglia. Everywhere teachers were establishing small boarding schools for two or three pupils. Educa-tion at these schools was more likely to be practical than liberal, and directed to the acquisition of skills rather than perspectives. Arithmetic and accounting were practical, and even mensuration and surveying seemed useful for the sons of landowners sensitive to matters of division and border. Navigation was popular too, not so much to teach boys to captain ships, but because it was the medium of progressive and current sciences. It gave a cultural focus to the science of angles, circles and time. Its problems opened up the principle mathematical issues of the day. In the mathematics of Mr. Tilney and Mr. Mack, William Gooch found a peculiarly relevant science for his social advancement. In the studious Gooch, Mr. Tilney and Mr. Mack found some reward for the hard times of village schoolmasters.

Flukey Pursuits

I had "found" the Brockdish Parish Register, the records of the Over-seers of the Poor, and William Gooch's will in the Norwich Public Records Office. "House Belong Memory" is the apt Solomon Islands pidgin name for their National Archives. Norwich was the last "House Belong Memory" I visited in my search for Gooch. I went there on a summer's day, forgetting the many people that now make History of their family trees and genealogies. I should have reserved a table two weeks earlier. Having come far, I waited till 3:00 P.M. when a table became free, only then to be told that the "search" for my documents would be made in the next hour. At 4:15 P.M. the "searcher" reported at my table that the documents were marked "fragile," and that I could not see what I wanted. "Never?," I asked, choking a little. "Not until they are repaired." "When will that be?" "Not in our lifetime."

I returned to Cambridge somewhat depressed. Evans-Pritchard suffering "Nueritis" in his tent, Malinowski hating "niggers" in his diary did not have it so bad, I thought. The Past is just another word for Other, and it is just as expensive to reach, just as costly on the nerves, just as unfathomable.

I wrote an ingratiating letter to the Keeper of the Records at Norwich. I had come ten thousand miles: perhaps I could pay to have the documents copied: perhaps I could hire an archivist to turn the pages. The Keeper's reply was prompt and generous. They had discovered that only the covers of the documents were fragile, not the documents themselves. I was welcome to reserve a table and see them.

4

HISTORY MADE

Of this time, Of this place

Tripos, as every Cambridge man is undoubtedly made to know, was originally the 16th century three legged-stool on which some "ould bachelor" sat like a clown and "wrangled" with the most acclaimed scholar on commencement day, as all received their degree from the university. It was a ritual of a reversed world, a sham to the scholar's seriousness and self-esteem. By association through the years, the tripos became the "ould bachelor" himself, Mr. Tripos, Mr. Three-Legged Stool. Mr. Tripos did not now wrangle but made a mocking, joking speech at the students who had wrangled or disputed in the Schools. Perhaps when clowns became scarce or when institutions became too self-important or when the reversed world came too close to the real one, the clowning act of Mr. Tripos was again transformed. By the 18th century it had become a bantering piece of Latin verse on the back of which was listed the year's successful candidates, Wranglers, in the order of merit in their public disputations in the Schools.

Tripos, as an instrument for making academic honors public, was still a sign of the ambivalences in judging learning, still a suggestion that the honors of academic institutions belonged not to life but to the game of life. It was still a mark of the joking relationship between the judges and the judged, the more binding and permanent for its levity and triviality. The Wranglers, *seriatim* from Senior or First to Twenty-first, as many as there were, would hold their title and place and the year of its achievement for the rest of their lives. William Gooch was Second Wrangler of 1791.

William Gooch is quoted twice in the *Oxford English Dictionary*. He shows how the word "wrangler" might be used. "I did above three times as much as the Sen[ior] Wrangler for last year." "I'm perfectly satisfied that the Senior Wranglership is Peacock's due." The learned compilers of the OED cite Christopher Wordsworth, *Scholae Academicae*. Wordsworth cited Gooch. The OED authors were shrewd in their shortcuts. They knew that the special language of Cambridge University was best discovered in the history of its customs. The antiquarians of academic institutions are the priests of all its rubrics, forever telling how things should be done properly, forever informing on the gloss of symbols, on the exegesis of texts for rituals and ceremony.

The last days of William Gooch at Cambridge held all his other days and were caught in the letters from which the *Oxford English Dictionary* quoted. In the "Sophs Schools," in the "Senate House Examinations," in his "Admission of the Questionists" Gooch was native of his time, native of his place. His "Acts," his "window papers," his "huddling" were theatre to the triumphs that made him Wrangler: not Senior Wrangler, that was Daniel Mitford Peacock, but Second Wrangler of 1791, for all time. The history he wrote of it was in letters to his "H^d Parents," William and Sarah Gooch. The letters are the source of my translation and inscription. One of them reads:

Nov. 6. 90

Cambridge

H^d Parents

I'm surpris'd I didn't mention the Hare, I know I intended it, & to have requested you to return my thanks to Mr. Pitts for it, as I saw it came from his by the Direction–I gave it to Brinkley–I'm sorry Mother you should make yourself uneasy about a Malady of which I was almost recover'd when I wrote last, & as I didn't feel my Health affected I'm vex'd with myself for mentioning it. However it is now entirely gone off, & certainly was never owing to any great exertion, as I don't practice any such violent exercise as you seem to imagine–Peacock kept a very capital Act indeed and had a very splendid Honour of which I can't remember a Quarter, however among a great many other things, Lax told him that "Abstruse and difficult as his Questions were, no Argument (however well constructed) could be brought against any Part of them, so as to baffle his inimitable Discerning & keen Penetration" &c.&c.&c.–However the Truth was that he confuted all the Arguments but one which was the 1st Opponent's 2nd Argument,–Lax lent him his assistance too, yet still he didn't see it, which I was much surpris'd at as it seem'd easier than the Majority of the rest of the Arg^s–Peacock with the Opponents return'd from the Schools to my Room to tea, when (agreeable to his usual ingenuous Manner) he mention'd his being in the Mud about Wingfield's 2nd argument, & requested Wingfield to read it to him again & then upon a little consideration, he gave a very ample answer to it.–I was third opponent only and came off with "optime quidem disputasti" i.e. "you've disputed excellently indeed" (quite as much as is ever given to a

third opponency–I've a first opponency for Novr 11th under
Newton against Wingfield & a second opponency for Novr 19th
under Lax against Gray of Peter-House. Peacock is Gray's first
opponent and Wingfield his third, so master Gray is likely to be
pretty well baited. His third Question (of all things in the world)
is to defend Berkley's immaterial system.

Mrs Hankinson & Miss Paget of Lynn are now at Cambridge.
I drank tea & supp'd with them on Thursday at Mr Smithson's
(the Cook's of S^t. Johns Coll.) & yesterday I din'd drank tea and
supp'd there again with the same Party, and today I'm going to
meet them at Dinner at Mr Hall's of Camb. Hankinson of Trin
(as you may suppose) have been there too always when I have
been there; as also Smithson of Emmanuel Coll. (son of this M^r
Smithson). Miss Smithson is a very accomplished girl, & a great
deal of unaffected Modesty connected with as much Delicacy
makes her very engaging.–She talks French, and plays well on
the Harpsichord. Mrs H. will continue in Camb. but for a day or
two longer or I should reckon this a considerable Breach upon
my Time;–However I never can settle well to any thing but my
Exercises when I have any upon my Hands, and I'm sure I don't
know what purpose 't would answer to fagg much at my Opponencies, as I doubt whether I should keep at all the better of the
worse they being upon subjects I've long been pretty well
acquainted with.–Yet I'm resolv'd when I've kept my first Opponency next thursday if possible to think nothing of my 2nd (for
friday se'nnight) till within a day or two of the time–One good
thing is I can now have no more, so I've the luck to be free from
the schools betimes, for the term doesn't end till the middle of
Dec^r–The only thing that remains to be determined about my
having Beevor of Ben'et (Nephew of Sr Thomas, as I think I
told you) is whether he comes to my Room an Hour in the day
or I go to his: for I understand by Chapman of Ben'et that he
expects me (contrary to all custom) to go to his, but he's
mistaken: every Body would then expect the same or have reason
to be affronted, and so I should be dancing about the Town
every day after my pupils, (as a french or Music-Master does for
3 guineas a Quarter) you would certainly blame me to submit to
this I don't doubt.–I mention'd it to Brinkley who is perfectly of
my opinion.–I expect one pupil from St Johns already (which is a
very likely college to afford me more)–I've written a Letter of
Thanks to Mr Mundy & inclosed the Copy.–I know nothing
more to say this time but that I am

Your ever dutiful Son

Willm Gooch

O,–I haven't look'd among my shirts yet–well, will you excuse
that for a few days.–I haven't told you neither that Smithson of
Emmanuel and I entertain'd the Ladies last night with fireworks.

Adieu.

In the year of 1791 there were twenty-one Wranglers on the tripos
list. Then there were twenty-two Senior Optimes, ranked, and sixteen
Junior Optimes, ranked. Unranked came the Hoi Polloi, the "pollmen"
who would receive their degrees with ritualistic formalism, who would
wrangle in a huddle on commencement day about absurdities–about
their own name, the name of their tutor–so that they could be said to
have performed the "Acts" or disputations demanded of them for their
degree by law. The Hoi Polloi went unhonored. They had their own
reversed world, however, in which by bravado and public show of
inconsequence they made their failures triumphs. The "Alphabet," they
would call themselves, or the "Rear Guard," or "Constant Quantity" or
"Suitors of the Muse," "Seven Wise Men," "Twelve Apostles." By that
they also made themselves native to their institution.

Among the Hoi Polloi of 1791 was a young man, more famous by far
than William Gooch. He was William Wordsworth. By being among the
Hoi Polloi, Wordsworth threw away all chance of fellowship in college,
preferment in the church or a place in law. The poet in him later
discovered the meaning of his crisis. He was "not of this time, not of this
place." His real education came not from institutions. He was native to
nature. To that, Acts, Sophs Schools, Tripos lists were not end, only
Prelude.

Of important days
Examinations, when the Man was weigh'd
As in the balance!–of excessive hopes,
Tremblings withal, and commendable fears,
Small jealousies, and triumphs good or bad....
Such Glory was but little sought by me,
And little won.

William Wordsworth made and remade poetic history of his experience at Cambridge in the *Prelude*. He had come as sizar, poor scholar
under patronage, to St. John's. Gooch had come as sizar to Gonville and

Caius. Wordsworth had come with advanced skills in mathematics, taught him by schoolmasters in his native north with their eye to his main chance at Cambridge. As Gooch had, too, but from East Anglia, the nursery for Caius scholars.

Wordsworth came to St. John's full of family calculations as to coming vacancies in the college fellowships only available to scholars from the north. Such fellowships would make his future assured. Gooch's calculations we do not know. But his letters were full of definitions of the situation. Becoming native to his institution, as we shall see, included familiarity with the options that his college life would offer. He gained a close knowledge of the ages of the fellows and of the vacancies among the fellows that would come with their marriage or their placement in a parish. Being a native academic was a very calculating business, full of the political knowledge both of college lore and college law.

"I was a freeman....It was enough for me to know I was otherwise endow'd," wrote Wordsworth. The emptiness of the external forms of learning at Cambridge contrasted with the fulness of his own real understanding. "I had a world about me, 'twas my own, I made it, for it liv'd for me." But that difference in himself might not be noticeable to an observer: "Each man was a memory to himself." The difference lay in the point of his soul "where we all stand single." Wordsworth felt he was "ill-tutored for captivity" in a "privileged world within a world." He did not have a "thirst for living praise, a reverence for the glorious dead." "The sight of these long vistas, catacombs in which perennial minds lie visibly entomb'd...have often stirr'd the heart of youth, and bred a fervent love of rigorous discipline. Alas! Such high commotion touch'd me not." Or so he thought. In the end he was as much a relativist as us all. "I cannot say what proposition is in truth the naked recollection of that time, and what may rather have been call'd to life by after meditation." William Gooch had little of William Wordsworth's sense of ambivalence, even in after-meditation.

Affecting Grandeur on a Small Scale

William Gooch was admitted to Gonville and Caius College at Michaelmas 1786. Caius ("Keys" as it was called) was founded twice: once in 1364 as Gonville, then in 1558 as Gonville and Caius. At Gooch's entry the College was on no crest of academic achievement. In the eighty years before his arrival, the publications of the resident fellows at Caius numbered only four sermons and a few verses. But a contemporary *Concise and Accurate Description of the University* could list, as former members of Caius, William Harvey, "discoverer of the circulation of the blood" and twenty-seven other eminent physicians, with the expectancy that the informed traveller would recognize their names.

The Master of Caius at the time of William Gooch's admission was Dr. John Smith, the Lowndean Professor of Astronomy. A friend described him as a "plain honest man of strong passions when moved. An eternal smoker of tobacco, pretends to a taste in painting, and may possibly understand it, though he looks as if he did not and has such an inarticulate way of expressing himself that only a few people understand what he says." Perhaps this inarticulateness was the reason why he never gave a lecture as Lowndean Professor for twenty-five years, a record only beaten by his successor, William Lax, whom we have already met in Gooch's letters and who never lectured for forty years. Nor did Dr. Smith, the Master of Caius, publish anything. He did erect a telescope on Caius parapets in the year he was appointed professor of astronomy, and he was a wiley academic politician. By 1786 he had fought many battles in the way of academic politics–with large principle over trivial matters and with foxy expedience. If he did not teach William Gooch much astronomy, he would do him service at the committee table: he was a member of the Board of Longitude and sparred with the equally foxy Sir Joseph Banks over Gooch's appointment to the Pacific.

Dr. John Caius, the second founder, was a man of monumental symbolism and historical determinism. He believed that the very shape of his college buildings was didactic of their purposes and worked hard to ensure that the shape of his institution would be reflected forever in the "cordial statutes" that he designed for it. Gonville College was already two-hundred years old when Dr. Caius remade it and added his name to it. He was Mary Tudor's physician and he never reformed his Catholicism. For that the Fellows of his own college hated him. While they could not loosen the bonds of the "preposterous government" that he had tied so well, when he died they destroyed the more supernumerary of his signs. They burned his "massing abominations" which "he termeth the college treasures." The doctor himself has ended up on the walls of his college chapel in a sarcophagus captioned "Fui Caius?" It would be interesting to hear from a symbolist such as he how the clutter of historic markers, accumulating through four centuries, might affect those who passed them by.

Dr. Caius had established his college with ceremony on 25 March 1558. It was the Feast of the Annunciation: Gonville was the Hall of the Annunciation. During the mass he offered the celebrating priest a *caduceus* ("the rod of prudent governance"), a cushion ("we give thee the cushion of reverence"), a salver ("this silver vessel with the letters patent and charter of foundation"), and a book of statutes ("the Book of Knowledge"). The next day he took the master, fellows and students for some prayers, some wine and merriment and a little exegesis. The College annalist wrote of his symbolizing:

Now the book indicates wisdom and knowledge and the cushion reverence, as has been explained in the statutes when the appointment of the master is prescribed. All the marks or signs of virtue are so inscribed on a shield that the two serpents with their tails entwined stand erect among the amarand, and leaning against the square stones of virtue with their breast sustain the book and with their head the sempervivium. To the shield succeeds a helmet, and to the helmet a dove, supporting a flower of amaranth, by which it may be known the letters are rendered acceptable by simple hearted wisdom. By these symbols he desired to intimate to the members of his college that letters and prudence being strengthened by the stone of virtue, they might thus arrive at immortality. In order that they might always have these symbols before their eyes he was careful to have them portrayed by pencil and called them the symbols of virtue.

The rod, the cushion, the book, the salver–and, of course, Dr. Caius in his sarcophagus–were all in the chapel when William Gooch arrived at the college in 1786. They were among the many everyday historical accoutrements of his college life. It has to be our assumption, born of our experience of symbols, that he saw them and he did not see them. He saw them every day of his life in college–twice a day in chapel service, each time he attended lectures there, in the examinations, during the weekly college declamations of thesis. One could imagine that he was audience to their exegesis in sermons, that he had been taught their significance in his first tour as a stranger to the college. Then he, when he was a more accustomed occupant of his environment, would have displayed them to other strangers. Between signs that are unseen for their ordinariness and signs unknown for their empty conventionality, where is History, where is the Past in the Present? The Past is the Present when we are entertained by it. The symbiosis of Past and Present is made in the reading or the contexting of the text of historical signs. Although the symbols that surround us might be seen with all the conventionality with which we see props on a stage, we reduce all the actions that take place before them to some drama from which we distil a meaning, an after-meditation that makes us see our symbols with knowing satisfaction. Out of this dialectic of convention and perception, History is born. Symbols precede and contextualize but hardly determine the actions.

Dr. Caius, the physician, had an eye for health when he built his college. He started a trend that other Cambridge colleges began to follow in leaving open one side of the college quadrangle for the sake of air, light and drainage. But he was more monumental than that in his symbolism. He built three gates for the college, through which students might daily or ceremonially pass: a Gate of Humility, a Gate of Virtue, a Gate of Honour. A student's life was meant to be a single passage through the humble acceptance of one's ignorance, through the acquisition of wisdom, to the public display of learning in the Schools and being honored for it. The Gate of Humility was low and simple, set off the public way; the Gate of Virtue gave access to the chapel, the library and the studies. The Gate of Honour grew in aptness through the centuries. The University built its Senate House directly opposite it. All the academic activities that brought students their honors were then held in the Senate House. The Gate of Honour was designed with more than a hint of Roman sepulchral dignity. It has been cited as one of the finer examples of Elizabethan Renaiisance architecture. Each of its hexagonal sides had a sundial and a weathercock.

The didactic message of Dr. Caius's monumental symbols was there for all to see. Most probably did see it. George Dyer, a contemporary of Gooch, wrote of the gates:

> Taking all together we may perhaps consider them as those little models of ships sometimes made by seafaring people to explain the sails, masts and different parts of a vessel; and we may gather from them some hints concerning their orders, and we may further, with advantage, bring away the moral sentiments which they are intended to convey. But we may approve of the utility of their instructions without admiring their architectural propriety. For to affect grandeur on so small a scale is not to be sublime.

George Dyer, if I could bend him to my cause, was suggesting that the conventionality of the signs might easily have been seen but that the full effectiveness was thwarted by their contradictions. The message of moral sublimity was somehow spoiled by the irony of their size. It does not take much to make symbols ambivalent. History inscribed in a landscape is free-running and full of wild notions.

Rhetorical Realities

Cambridge University at the end of the 17th century was, as the phrase has gone, "unreformed." "Reformation" like Wordsworth's *Prelude*, is often an after-meditation, born of some ritual or dramatic act that catches process with the rhetoric of stucture and change. Cambridge University was reformed by Royal Commission in 1852, but there was plenty of dissent of a reforming kind, both radical and conservative, in the years 1786-1791. There was radical dissent from subscription, the

A

B

C

FIGURE 6: (A) GONVILLE AND CAIUS COLLEGE. (B) DR. JOHN CAIUS.
(C) GATE OF HONOUR.

oath of loyalty to the Church of England required of every graduate. But there was as well conservative alarm at unitarian unorthodoxy and "congregations" of "silly indigent female paupers." Fox-hunting parsons, absentee priests and wealthy bishops raised a social conscience and a protest here and there, but most of Cambridge lived by the worldly wisdom of patronage in college and in church.

Mathematics was thought by some to be "as useless for clergymen and lawyers as it would be useful for a carpenter and a joiner." But many thought with Isaac Newton's teacher, Gilbert Wakefield, "what subject of human contemplation shall compare in grandeur with that which demonstrates the trajectories, the periods, the distances, the dimensions, the velocities and gravitation of the planetary system; states the tides...contemplates the invisible comet, wandering in his parabolic orb for successive centuries...? Language sinks beneath the contemplation so exalted, and so well calculated to inspire the most awful sentiment of the Great Artificer." The privilege of the aristocracy roused rage, but so did the ostentation of the newly rich, the "Indian Nabobs." It was a time of revolution, French and American. It was also the occasion of the centenary of the English Glorious Revolution. Constitutional societies were spawned by current politics and celebratory history to debate corruption and reform. William Pitt was Cambridge's member of parliament and seemed to have sold his liberal soul for power. He caught in his person and in his every speech Cambridge's torture in living *realpolitik* with high ideals.

High ideals were everywhere expressed and perhaps for that reason as heard and unheard as the monumental symbolism of Dr. Caius was seen and unseen. But rhetorical declarations about what the university was were not so much descriptions as affirmations of what the university "really was." The realism of an ideal past that had never been was paraded as if it were an actual present. Samuel Parr made the high ideals as plain as any. The university, he said in 1787 in a sermon, corrected singularity and forwardness by promoting the debates of minds with minds in a place where different classes lived together under a system of general discipline. The university's established rules produced habits of regularity and decorum. It laid a strong yoke on the impetuosity of youth. It cultivated honor as a natural sentiment, gave a generous sense of shame and a selfless propensity of heart. There was a goodly effect on the "temper as well as the taste by the daily and hourly view of edifices, agreeable from convenience or striking from magnificence, or venerable from antiquity." "Pictures, statues, inscriptions, public harangues and other local circumstances may excite in men of vivid conceptions and glowing ambitions, not merely to admire, but to perpetuate and to share in the celebrity of places adorned through many successive ages, by many bright luminaries of the schools, the pulpit, the bar and the temple."

The past caught in its environmental signs and in its performances was, for Samuel Parr, the effective expression of what the university was. The signs that it was otherwise were only appearances, insignificant, accidental. The *realpolitik* of the idealist was to wink at contradictions, to see intriguing formalism as play not as fraud. The *realpolitik* of the reformer was to see the real Cambridge in the emptiness of its signs. In this view the clowning tripos, the pointless huddling to fulfil statutory requirements, the conniving arbitration of what was law were the sacraments of decadence. But to see the reality behind the shams or to see the shams as the reality required equal inventiveness.

There was a sense that Cambridge was an institution of cliched signs. And by that it was unreformed, its rhetoric empty, its public systems of signs static. But it is difficult to believe that Pasts were static while Presents are process. If we have a sense that culture is both invention and prescription, then History made of what actually happened in the past must surely describe what metaphors were made of cliches. Stain a living cell and see the structures of a dead cell. Stamp Gooch's soul with the cliches and the rhetoric of Cambridge's unreform, and there is no window on who he was at all.

Metaphors and Cliches

William Gooch came as "sizar" to Caius. It was the first cliche in his Cambridge life. The word sizar is presumed to be derived from "sizes," the portions of food or "commons" that the sizar freely received from his college. Over the centuries, sizars had been poor boys working for their education by being the private servants of the master and fellows, or the public servants of the college. In a world largely mapped by the tables at which one ate, the sizars had no table of their own, only the table and the left-over food of the fellows they served. They wore a distinctive gown. They were recognizable and located wherever they went. Not they alone, of course: the university and the colleges were places of set relationships, known in a mark of dress or in the application of a rule. Between masters, senior fellows, junior fellows, fellow commoners, bachelors, scholars, pensioners and sizars there were sharp boundaries. The boundaries were made sharper by the cliched past that described the differences as they used to be rather than defined their current roles. So fellow-commoners, usually the sons of aristocrats, were a class apart. They enjoyed their privileges of status and wealth by eating at the fellows' table, by clowning at their studies but having every legalism and formalism of the institution bent in their favor. They were very distant in social position from sizars, who, having won their place by talent and patronage, would cling to it by winning the academic prizes and filling the academic vacancies. By that the sizars became the university and colleges of another generation of fellow-commoners. There was symbiosis in their ironies.

All the roles, not just the sizars', held the images of the past as to what those roles were, and by that held some contradiction and grievance in the present. For sizars to wear the "livery of a pauper" when all around thought themselves gentlemen and scholars was to play a role out of season with the times of the institution. The colleges at Cambridge in Gooch's days were in-between the earlier times, centuries long, when inmates were comfortable with divisions and boundaries that mirrored those of a society outside and a time, coming in the 19th century when college life would be something different–when, by initiation and communal activity in sport and education, college days were made liminal to life. In that liminality relationships could be different, social boundaries could be differently set. In Gooch's days the colleges were in-between, unreformed.

By William Gooch's time at Caius the physical separation and menial tasks of sizars had disappeared. They ate with the pensioners (the students who paid their fees) and no longer served the fellows. The last of their tasks of being "bible clerks" and looking after the chapel had been shuffled off at their own request in 1767. This freedom was duly registered in the college *Gesta*, the custom book where every adjustment of boundary and ceremonial regularity was entered. Indeed sizarship, as in Gooch's case, had been reduced to a temporary period in which the sizar, accepted in the college, studied to win a bursary and by that became a scholar. The colleges had become wealthy in the 18th century. Their student numbers had declined during the century, but in Gooch's days had begun to rise again. Any young man with talent and application might become a scholar, that is, earn a scholarship. Sizars were recipients of college wealth: scholars mediated it. Gooch, by becoming scholar entered the means and relations of production of his institution, and, by that, was made native to his time and place.

This can be seen in the "Copy of my Bill at College to Xmas 1787" among Gooch's papers. He had entered the college as sizar in May 1786. He won his way to scholar in September 1787. The accounting is from September (Michaelmas) 1786 to Michaelmas 1787, with his expenses carried through to Christmas 1787.

Receiv'd

Scholarship to Lady 87	£ 4.	9.	6
Lady Middleton's Bounty	20.	0.	0
S^r. J^n. Berney's Do.	5.	5.	0
Scholarship to Mich. 87	4.	13.	2

Total Income	£ 34.	7.	6
Total Expenses	28.	9.	1

Balance due to Mr Gooch	£ 5.	18.	7

Gooch's income came from three sources–a bounty from Lady Middleton, a bursary from Sir Jonathon Berney and an unnamed scholarship of the college. The first letter of William Gooch's collection of "Letters, Memoranda" is one of thanks to Lady Middleton. The letter to Lady Georgiana Middleton of Middleton Hall, Warwickshire, is in rough copy in Gooch's cipher of Greek letters. Perhaps only the rough copy was in "Greek," or perhaps a "Greek" letter was sent to his benefactress as a shy compliment to her education and status or as a display of a new skill for which she was paying. In the rough copy he experimented several times with his signature; and there are other signs of self-conscious rehearsal in this gesture of deference. Lady Georgiana was the daughter of the wealthy Evelyn Chadwick of Notts and widow of Thomas Willoughby, Lord Middleton. She was greatly generous to education in her county. Probably she had no specific or personal interest in Gooch, but there was a social network in patronage, and perhaps there was a connection between her and Thomas Maynard (Hesilrige) of Gooch's own village of Brockdish. In any case, Gooch became practiced in his use of the networks. The £20 bounty of Lady Middleton remained his all his stay at Cambridge. Lady Middleton married Edward Miller Mundy of Shipley Hall, at Ilkeston, Derbyshire in 1788 but died within eighteen months. Mundy was member of Parliament for Derbyshire. He seems to have had a fairly casual interest in politics, if his total silence on matters reported in Parliament was any sign. He continued his wife's bounty to Gooch. At the end of his studies, Gooch wrote a letter to Mr. Mundy–in English script–saying at the end

of his student career what he had said to Lady Middleton at its beginning, that his best show of gratitude was to be the conscientious student.

Five guineas came to Gooch from the £200 endowed to Caius College
by Sir John Berney on his death in 1782. The Berney family, deeply
rooted in Norfolk, had close association with Caius. Sir John himself had
been a fellow of the college. The other unnamed grant of £4/13/2 no
doubt belonged to those secret funds which college bursars providen-
tially produce with both reluctance and surprise. The bursar of Caius
was Richard Fisher. He changed his name to Belward in 1791 and later
became master of the college. He was Gooch's tutor, and they seemed to
enjoy a mutual confidence. Gooch, later faced with expenses for his
Pacific voyage, would gain credit through Belward and the college.
Belward would also be broker for other grants in the scavenging life
Gooch thought he was about to begin.

How much Gooch was mediator of the endowments to the college can
be seen from his expenses. He was housed in Gonville, the oldest of the
college buildings. It is the judgement of the great architectural historian
of Cambridge, Robert Willis, that Caius students at this time enjoyed the
comfort of individual bed-studies, that each, at least in the newer wings
had a carrel of a monastic sort in his room. We see Gooch from his
accounts furnishing his room with feather bed and fire-irons and kettle
and drapery. He had a joiner do £6/2/0 worth of joining, costing more
than either his college stipend or Sir John Berney's scholarship. Cobbler
and tailor made his clothes. The grocer provisioned food for the suppers
in his rooms when he acted host, and the cook billed him for meals
delivered to him when others acted host to him. The butler, his
bedmaker, his launderess were his daily servants.

William Gooch rose a class by managing his money. No doubt the
butler and the bedmaker joined the cook and the grocer in the
conspiracy of recognizing Gooch's managerial gestures "as if" they were
real, while reserving their true deferences for those who counted. But
class is catching, and when William Gooch sailed to the Pacific on a
much larger pension, the Brockdish barber's son took the Brockdish
innkeeper's son as servant. Never mind that they would look at one
another somewhat awkwardly the whole voyage long, neither knowing
how to play their roles. Scholarship money made Gooch a worldly entre-
preneur with his material things. It gave him practice in upward social
mobility.

All told, there were 116 students at Caius from Gooch's first days to
his last. We know the occupations of the fathers of a hundred of them.
We know what ninety-eight of the students themselves became. Of the
fathers, thirty-three were priests, three baronets, twenty-four gentlemen,
twelve farmers, three grocers, one furrier, one tanner, three mercers,
four attorneys, three schoolmasters, six surgeons, three wooldrapers, one

mariner, one ironmonger, one vintner. And there was one hairdresser, old William Gooch. Seventy-eight of the students became priests. Then there were seven physicians among them, two lawyers, three army officers, two sheriff alderman, one gentleman, one diplomat, two baronets, one professor. And there was one short-lived astronomer.

The statistics are a tease. It is difficult to say what sort of "social fact" they are. The trading classes are as represented as the gentry in the college. Perhaps a hairdresser's son was more distant than any from a baronet's son. Perhaps Gooch was reminded of his origins more often than the tanner's or ironmonger's or vintner's sons: the daily primping of hair and wig before the noon meal called for a barber. Gooch's friends–those he mentions in his letters–were all from other colleges, Trinity, Emmanuel, St. John's. Perhaps there is a hint in that of his social awkwardness at Caius. There were many students–Wordsworth among them–who saw sizarship as a mark of social humiliation. Many deplored the flaunted decadence of the fellow-commoners and their cliques, and berated the effeminacy and violence of upper class Cambridge life. Published memoirs of the times caught the posing. There is no sense of contradiction in William Gooch's contentment in his role, however. He seemed to make metaphors of his cliches very easily.

Encompassing a World

In the late 18th century Cambridge University had not yet got over Isaac Newton's *Principia* of 1683 and John Locke's *Essays on Human Understanding* of 1689. With Newton's declaration of the principles of order in nature and Locke's propositions for a mechanics of morality, Cambridge had in hand a normal science that made sense of every expression of human understanding, in classical texts, in mathematical theorems, in moral philosophy, in theological speculation. Natural order and utility were the light by which all could be read. And when William Paley wrote his *Principles* in 1783, Cambridge had a crib on its own *mentalité*. The *Principles* were a sort of *Summa* of prudential morality. All political, religious, social and moral life was divided into sets of manageable theorems that left the world as it was with comfortable orthodoxy and stylish reasoning. It was a volume made for "fagging," the world encompassed by bits and pieces.

With Newton, Locke and Paley in hand, Cicero, Lucian, Homer, Tully, Demosthenes, Sophocles, Virgil and Quintilian became mirrors for utilitarianism. No need for artfulness or conspiracy in moulding minds, when the writings of the ancients on friendship, authority and nature's harmony made natural sense. No need to maintain that Latin and Greek grammars were not tedious. Swotting then, as now, blunted comprehension. *mentalité* is not a matter of genius. Relevance, and the concurrence of current and ancient thinking, came with merging their sets of meanings in translating. Student studies and student minds were full of short cuts and cribs on the cribs of their *mentalité*. No need for brilliance. Hoi Polloi and Wrangler were much the same. It was performance of their learning–rather than its substance–that made for orthodoxy and cultured acceptance.

The Schools–the formal occasions of disputation–were made for making *mentalité*: they were made for normal science. In the Schools, some proposition out of established understanding was abstracted and defended against an opposition that had no context other than its own self-contained logic. *"Recte statuit Paleius de criminibus et poenis"* declaimed the defendant, or the "Act" as he was called in performance. "Paley's arguments about capital punishment are correct." *"Non recte statuit Paleius de criminibus et poenis,"* his opponent would respond. "Paley's arguments about crime and punishment are not correct." *"Probo. Si, qui Facinus in se admittit, Poenas isti facinorii adjudicatans pendere debet, cedit quaestio."* "I prove my point. If a judge must condemn a man to hang who has pleaded guilty, then Paley's argument fails." And so the Opponent began a string of eight or five or three syllogisms, collected from a hoard of such strings that had been published or archived away by some informal league of opponency. Creativity in such syllogisms was dangerous: it might deflect the defendant from making the expected distinctions and leave the opponent inventing further syllogisms on his feet. The proper response of the defendant to the syllogism was either a denial or a distinction made between what was acceptable or unacceptable in the opponent's argument. An unexpected denial or an idosyncratic distinction set the dog-Latin in the opponent's mind chasing the hares in the defendant's head, an unpleasant experience for both. So, disputation done in public was not discursive. It was a performance of systems of knowledge. The systems were hardened by the awkwardness of pidgin Latin and the tensions of the staged nature of the disputation. It was as conventional as a duel or a joust.

Into such conventionality, the freedom of science and the ambiguities of new understanding did not easily fit. *"Recte statuit Newtonius de...Recte statuit Lockeius de...Recte statuit Paleius de...."* The defense of Newton, Locke and Paley made for theorems and learned normality. Cambridge, in any case, seems to have been left with the dark side of Newton's brilliant efflorescence, his xenophobia and his private jealousy for his public knowledge. Where on the continent mathematicians were inspired by Newton to new discoveries, at Cambridge they learned him like a creed. Not that the mathematicians were unaccomplished or unexcited: the mathematics was applied. If nature might have a mathematical dimension, then air and water, stars and earth were a laboratory just by being measurable, just for the puzzle they made in being quantified. Hydrostatics, fluxions, optics, mechanics–by the very invention of their names–became separable domains that might be mastered and managed and displayed. "Resolution of quadratic, cubic and biquadratic equations," "conic sections," "rectifying of curves," "process of equinox," "Lunar theory" became coded expressions of practical problems that needed to be resolved, became terms for defined parts of a universe that could be appropriated. That there was some discrepancy between the conventionality of disputation and the unconventionality of scientific discovery was something sensed at Cambridge. The reformers, in the last decades of the 18th century, urged examination rather than disputation as a more appropriate instrument of education. By 1790-91 when William Gooch was performing his Acts and doing his Senate House examinations, the processes of discovering a new balance between performance and testing had been underway for ten or fifteen years. Paper was also becoming relatively less expensive, and the wealth of nations was going a little more into books. Samuel Vince, the old boy of Harleston and Gooch's shining example, for all the scorn that the historians of mathematics might pour on him for his lack of scholarly advance, was experimental with printed texts and prospectuses of his teaching syllabus. It was a time of encyclopedias and easily available translations of new discoveries into general forms of knowledge.

As he prepared for his Pacific Voyage, William Gooch went unerringly to such summaries of practical knowledge in medicine, geography, religion, language, as well as astronomy and mathematics. His mood was never one of mystery, only of confidence that something learned was something solved. "I want you to promise," he wrote to his father, "to let me give you a lecture every day regularly on popular astronomy, when I come home.–Nothing is more easy to comprehend, and I'm convinc'd you'll think it entertaining after the first two or three lectures.–You will then know what I am about when abroad, and will have a clear idea (from the lats and longs of the places) how we reckon time, etc. (for in every diff. longitude the time of noon is different), and a hundred other little things which you would like to know, you wd then be able to find out."

If, in the stirrings of change at Cambridge in these years, there was a growing consciousness of the intransigence of Schools and science and if disputations were experiencing a last flourish, there was also a more recognizable modern entrepreneurial spirit moving. It was to be seen in small things: the development of printed examinations for the mathematical tripos and an extravagance in the use of paper in answering of them. The cost of the Schools system had been its human time. Now there was a sense–and young Gooch would catch it as he spent extravagantly on travel and materials to become the "astronomer on board the *Daedalus*"–that the cost of learning belonged somehow outside self, in material things as means to ends.

From the books Gooch took with him to the Pacific and from the lists of the books his father sold after his death, we can enumerate the texts he had in hand and merge them with the syllabi of readings that have been recorded for Caius. He read Lucian and Tully in first year, Homer and Demosthenes in second, Sophocles, Cicero, Virgil, Quintilian in third and fourth year. Newton, Locke and Paley he read through four years. He also studied a whole range of specialist treatises: among them, Whiston on *Euclid*, Milne on *Conic Sections*, Simpson on *Geometry*, Emerson on *Mechanics*, Simpson's *Fluctions*, Parkinson's *Mechanics*, Hellins's *Essentials*, Vince's *Process of Equinox*, Mayer's *Lunar Theorem*, Cotes's *Mathematical Lectures*. These were the texts he had in hand, not by any means all those he studied. It would be fair to say that Gooch read much more widely. The formalism of the syllabus did not lighten the burden. John Brinkley, Senior Wrangler of 1788, had studied twelve to fourteen hours a day to win his honor. Gooch would have had plenty of reminders of that.

While the methods of measuring and examining were changing at the end of the 18th century, what was being measured was not. Cambridge University was enormously entertained by its yearly batch of questionists at the end of their degree. From May 1786 when he entered Caius to September 1790 when he began his final year, William Gooch's academic attention was largely focussed on his college. He had read his Latin and Greek texts and been examined in them within the college. He had practiced his defenses and his opponencies in weekly sessions in the chapel. He had taken his turn at Latin declamations. In all these, and through the years, he was tested and ranked by his college tutors. They would know their champions and would be eyeing those of other colleges. By their reckoning it was better to have first wranglers in successive years than to have two of their own competing in the one year. So tactics were matters of counsel with their students and ploy among themselves. The tutors eyed the proctors and the moderators in their rounds of office; these would be the officers of the university who would conduct the Acts and Senate-house examinations. In the politics of knowlege, it was necessary to know whose champions were where and the prejudices of their judges.

At the end of three years, the students were already implicitly graded into potential Wranglers, Optimes and Hoi Polloi. As the final year began, September 1790 for William Gooch, the proctors asked the colleges for their lists of "hard reading," and "non-reading" men. Only the "hard reading" men would perform in the Schools. "Non-reading" men were those who had opted out of mathematics and would only compete in prizes for classics. Or they were those, like the Hoi Polloi, who had measured their academic engagement more narrowly. With the men of the final year across the colleges thus roughly graded, the entertainment lay in establishing the ranking of students within each. The last rites of making natives to the university were begun.

The lists of "hard-reading" men given to the moderators triggered procedures whose rubrics were less a rule of institution than webs of significance for the participants. Certain things had to be done. William Lax of Trinity and Thomas Newton of Jesus were the moderators of 1791. They chose the Acts who were ceremoniously notified of their obligation to defend within two weeks. Within hours the Act had to return a note marking three questions he would defend. We do not know what William Gooch's theses were. We can guess that they were conservative: in his letter to his "H^d Parents" he said of Master Gray, "His third question (of all things in the world) is to defend Berkleys immaterial system." We have, however, a list of the propositions Caius students defended at the time: various sections of Newton's *Principia*; Cotes on centripetal force; Halley on the determination of solar parallax; Morgan on mechanical forces; Locke on "Can matter think?"; Paley on penalties, on happiness, on promises; Berkeley on sight and touch; and Montesquieu's laws. Two of the three questions to be defended were usually mathematical; one was philosophical. The moderators would enter the three questions in the register and then send them out to the three opponents who would provide eight, five and three arguments respectively against them.

The Acts and Opponents had waited for the privilege and the pain of their performance. They had learned by watching and then they were pleasurably bound by their distinctiveness. The Act was privileged with a *dormiat* or sleep-in. His preparation was supposedly so intense that he must work late and sleep through morning chapel. His making of an exception to the rule was a sign of how much he was native to it. The very essence of his monastic, institutional, college life was not the regularity but the exception: "feasts" when he alone might have a tart for commons; a fire in the dining room. The institution made a boundary round him while he made a boundary against the institution. A *dormiat* needed or not, was the mark of being the Act. He would take it self-consciously, and he would be seen to take it. An Act had to do all other things properly, too; he had to "wine" his opponents, to lessen the possibility of mistakes on the day, and be "wined" in turn when it was over.

On the day of the Acts themselves, the moderators would process to the Sophs Schools behind the bedell with the book of the university's statutes. It was a sign of the real presence of the institution. Occasionally Acts had to cease in the middle of an argument when the real presence was required elsewhere. The moderator from his dais on the back wall, the defendants and opponents to his right and left facing one another from their pulpits, would begin the Acts on the hour of three. The Acts would last a little over an hour. William Lax in the year of William Gooch's Acts sent a ripple through tradition by allowing them to continue for two hours. He changed tradition, too, by enlarging the formulaic judgements of moderators–"*optime disputasti*" ("you disputed excellently")–to long encomiums. It was his way of getting into the act and making Acts flourish. Gooch reported Lax as saying of Peacock, "Abstruse and difficult as his Questions were, no argument (however well constructed) could be brought against any Part of them, so as to baffle its inimitable Discerning and keen Penetration." "Etc., Etc., Etc.," added Gooch.

If one were Thomas Aquinas or William of Occam, one wrangled with freelance brilliance, reeling syllogisms out of a disciplined mind, creating distinctions out of a logical thesis. If one were a lesser breed, a sophister, say, in the final year of a degree, one wrangled much more by rote, in terror lest the defendant, either by ignorance or by brilliance, offer an unforeseen distinction, fearful that the opponent would respond with some surprise. Tongue-tied by Latin and by the rubrics of logic, exposed to an audience that winked and laughed in nervous sympathy, the focus of the Wrangler's mind was on show. His creativity was evanescent: come and gone in a tidy phrase; he was mercenary to a thesis not his own.

The result of the Acts in November and December, by parley of the moderators with the college tutors, was a preliminary classing. Now those to be admitted to the degree were divided into eight classes: groups one and two would be potential Wranglers, three and four Senior Optimes, five and six Junior Optimes, seven and eight Hoi Polloi. The listings were posted two days before the examinations which began on Plough Monday after the Epiphany, a little over a week into January. The examinations, Monday through Thursday of that week, were a gruelling sorting and ranking of each student in his class. It was a time of great intensity and, as Wordsworth put it, of "small jealousies." When candidates were paired and pitted against one another, ideals of fairness clashed with college loyalties. Gooch complained of Lax's treatment of him, but made a "very particular request" of his parents that they not mention his concern to anybody. In being native to his institution he had to practice his "wink upon a wink upon a wink."

Two hundred years of cultural evolution from the 18th century have given us a model of what true examination should be. We are used to the paraphernalia of judgement and fair play. We know all the cultural tricks that separate examiners from examinees, and examinees from one another. We are practiced, as in a puberty rite, as to how individual knowledge should be tested. The Senate House examinations were not quite like our model. They need something of an anthropological sense of difference to understand them.

Plough Monday, the first day of the examinations, began in the colleges with a breakfast. Breakfast, at the time, was not a communal meal, so this was special, out of the ordinary. The "Father" of the college was the president of the meal. He then led the questionists in procession to the Senate Hall. In the Senate Hall the eight classes were arranged at three large tables. The first six classes were at two tables, the Hoi Polloi at the third. At each of the tables sat two examiners who read out a question to their students. The questionists wrote their answers in English, and, when one was finished, another question was read. The examiners marked the papers as they were written. There were three sessions of examinations in the day, 9:30-11:00 A.M., 1:00-3:00 P.M., 3:30-5:00 P.M. Then, in the evening from 7:00-9:00 P.M., the first two classes of Wranglers visited the senior moderators in their private rooms or in the Combination Room of the college to be set more problems. At all sessions, questionists might be called away from the table to be queried by a moderator or a "Father" of a college. The two classes of Wranglers would be sent to the "window," that is, private tables, where they worked out problems from a paper in script or print. Mondays and Tuesdays were given to mathematics. Wednesday was given to natural religion and moral philosophy. By Thursday the moderators and the various "Fathers" had made preliminary rankings in each of the classes. There would be some, as Gooch in his letter said of himself and Peacock, *in equilibrio*, not yet separated. Thursday was devoted to judging between candidates *in equilibrio*, establishing "brackets" or groupings within classes, so that a *magnum intervallum* might divide groups of Wranglers. These brackets would then be examined to separate individuals within them. Then often late into Thursday night, as was the case with Gooch when John Brinkley brought the news, the tripos list would be announced.

Through all these four days, special rites surrounded the questionists: food and wine in the combination room, (usually out of bounds to them), additions to "commons" from a college benefactor, meetings in tutors' studies to discuss outcomes, privileges in avoiding a range of daily obligations. The social space of being a questionist was the limen of any *rite de passage*. In the special language, in the privileged exception to ordinary rule, in the new relationship between the student and his tutors, there were many signs that said that the questionist was in-between, that he was in a space where all the signifiers of who he was and who he was going to be might be most clearly read. In institutions of the monastic kind–I think of colleges and naval vessels–the occasions of privilege and exception are the moments of greatest control. There is none so native to his institution as he who guards its custom of exception.

The Senate House Examinations were a period of extraordinary intensity. The plums of academic life ripened at this seasonal moment. The questionists knew that the structures of their future lives were being made and they knew very precisely how they should behave; they knew the forms and the shams. They knew how the examinations worked and how they "really" worked. When the classes were posted on Plough Monday, two days before the examinations, the students knew they had a choice. On Gooch's tripos list, for example, Wingfield (who tripped up Peacock in the Acts) and Gray (who surprisingly defended Bishop Berkeley,) "gulphed it," took an *aegrotat*, when they discovered they were in the Wrangler's class. That is, they either reckoned that the examinations were not worth the risk of losing their class or that receiving a more precise ranking was not worth the toil. So they discovered some reason of ill-health to take out what honors they already had. It was a bargain that the institution made with a wink. *Aegrot* then appeared beside their unranked names on the tripos list. By that choice, they also gave up a chance at a fellowship. For the rest, fellowships were almost assured. Nineteen of the twenty-two Wranglers of 1791 became fellows of different colleges.

After the posting of the tripos, a questionist became a "Bachelor." It was a step between the noviceship of a student's life and the profession of fellows. But Gooch showed in his letters at the time of the Acts that he bore some of the badges of profession a little before. He told his "H^d Parents" how he was to tutor a student named Beevor of Ben'et and that he expected he would have more students from St. John's. No doubt even before the Acts and the Senate House Examinations, Gooch had won fame enough to attract the attention of students wanting to conquer the system. "Pupil-mongering," the reformers of Cambridge called it. They saw it as a symptom of the university's failure at effective education. Private entrepreneurial tutoring might be a very utilitarian response to the vocational problem of getting high ranks of the tripos list, but it underscored the ineffective tutoring and lecturing of the colleges. That larger philosophical issue did not worry Gooch. He was a very utilitarian young man. He had another problem. Gooch was son of a barber; Beevor was nephew of a baronet. The student, it seems, expected Gooch to tutor him in his rooms at Ben'et. To Gooch it was a moment of entertainment to the meaning of his role. He would not "be dancing about town every day after my pupils (as a french or music master does for three guineas a quarter)." "You would certainly blame me to submit to this I don't doubt," he wrote to parents who, he clearly thought, were watching the proprieties and etiquettes of their socially mobile son very closely. Brinkley–the other famous son of Brockdish–always ready to coach on these matters was of the same opinion.

It was not a matter of importance, but being ordinary it was a matter
of large significance. Beevor and Gooch were entertained by the significance of a walk to one another's rooms. The direction of one to the
other was a sign of deference–to aristocratic status or to academic role.
The actions were drama. They made a metaphor of status and authority.
The pair were agreed that a walk between rooms, which on any other
occasion might be friendly or casual, in this instance played out the
structure of their relationship. The enlarged meaning was public:
Brinkley saw it; Gooch's parents will see it; Chapman, Beevor's friend
who carried the request to Gooch, saw it. There was an audience who
would know that in this first act of a tutor all other acts were contained.
There was a common sense that if he lost this confrontation he lost or
would lose them all. That common sense is History at work making a
Present. The enlarged meaning of the actions showed the invention: a
walk was a ritual of deference. The agreed meaning showed the given
code, the common sense. The participants were quite free to see it
otherwise yet were bound to its reality at the same time. In the kit of
their common sense, they had compromises that would resolve the
contradictions: they could act as if things were otherwise, meet in a third
place, meet alternatively in one another's room. Their inventions could
take them in any direction, save changing the sense of the realism of
their "as if" worlds.

When Ash Wednesday came, Gooch was ready to be made a bachelor.
He was called down from the gallery of the Senate House with the other
questionists of the tripos list. On the floor of the Senate, his college
bedmaker put a rabbit-fur hood over his head: it was his "hoodling."
Why his bedmaker? I really cannot say. But then why does mother's
brother perform a circumcision? Why move from left to right in puberty
ceremonies? "Because it is our custom," "Because it is the proper thing to
do." "Because it looks right." In the kaleidoscope of symbols in ritual
action, it is their pattern that makes sense. It is the pattern of signs that
is sacramental more than their separate symboling. That the bedmaker,
the most menial of Gooch's servants, yet the master of ceremonies of the
material aspect of his college life, should assist at his first academic
robing "looked right." It fitted the ironies of what was to come in the
conferring when the university seriously clowned its way through its
most important display of itself. It fitted the ironies that had already
happened in the tripos.

Assembled on the floor of the Senate and arrayed in their hoods, the
questionists took their oath to the Church of England from the School-
keeper. They "subscribed." Since they had all taken their turns to
defend William Paley's thesis "On Subscription," they probably were all,
like him, unable to "afford a conscience." They subscribed to all the
privileged future that would be theirs, because they chose to be silent on

the contradictions of faith and learning, on the conflicts of privilege and freedom. Their whole acculturation was expressed in the breath of their oath. It came and went quickly. There had been no Romanists or Dissenters at Caius since Dr. Caius's turbulent times. In 1791, they were not expected.

On the Senate House floor after the oath, the "Fathers" presented the questionists as their "sons" and these "children" were reprimanded and condemned. The Bedell knocked on the door to subdue their rowdiness. Then they were taken to the Sophs Schools to "huddle for their degree" and giddily enact the absurdities of their mock Acts. When these were finished they were "bachelors."

By these last days of his Admission to the Degree in January 1791, William Gooch was on his way to something and somewhere else. In his letter of 6 November 1790 he mentioned a visit to Mr. Smithson's, the cook at St. John's. He wrote how he dined and drank tea there several times. "Miss Smithson," he wrote, "is a very accomplished girl, and a great deal of unaffected modesty connected with as much delicacy makes her very engaging–She talks french and plays well on the harpsichord." There was a postcript. "I haven't told you neither that Smithson of Emmanuel and I entertained the ladies last night with fireworks. Adieu!"

A Small Lien on Otherness

Sally Smithson entered William Gooch's life only to say goodbye. His bachelor's ceremonies over in March, he was gone on the *Daedalus* in August. Sally, with her mother, followed him to London to see him packed, then to Gravesend to catch his sailing, down to Portsmouth for a farewell, even to the Isle of Wight on the chance that winds would blow to their advantage and they would have another meeting. Gooch, who till this time had presented himself and made his History, to his parents, now quietly turned to Sally as his audience. Even if he addressed his letters to his mother and father, it was Sally to whom he wrote. By the time he was writing long journal-letters on the *Daedalus*, his subterfuges were gone. He was then confident that his trivia, affectionately recorded, would be affectionately read.

As astronomer and navigator on the *Daedalus* Gooch's concerns were for time and distance. In his letters to Sally, his new science became a traveller's trick. He measured their slowly differing hours and, by imagining, joined her in her time. In the days before he left and as the length of his voyaging dawned on them all, he buoyed Sally and his parents with the promise that at worst he would be gone no more than four years, at best no more than three. He instructed his father on birthday greetings to Sally. His father, ever accountant of his own duties, put the birthday greetings on file in his son's papers. It was to be one birthday greeting only. By the time of the second, they knew the voyage would never end.

The last year of William Gooch's life was full of foreign experiences. The first was Sally. "Goody Two-Shoes," he called her. It seems intrusive to ask why. In any case their secret has gone with them. "Goody Two-Shoes" was a character in a very small book with a very large title.

> The History of Little Goody Two-Shoes; otherwise called Mrs Margery Two-Shoes with the means by which she acquired her learning and wisdom and in consequence thereof her estate; set forth at large for the benefit of those who from a state of rags and care and having shoes by half a pair their fortune and their face would fix and gallop in a coach and six. See the original manuscript in the Vatican at Rome and the cuts by Michael Angelo. Illustrated with the comments of one of our great modern critics.

Miniature volumes for small children were the practice of the day. The lessons of the stories, however, were larger and for a more adult eye. *Little Goody Two-Shoes* first appeared in 1765. Its anonymous author was probably Oliver Goldsmith. Certainly the story of how farmer Graspall threw the Meanwells off their property, thus making little Margery and her brother wandering poor, was one of Goldsmiths' preoccupations. There was little romance and much satire in the telling of how Margery bettered herself after a gift of two shoes, became President of ABC College and in the end became Lady Jones, endowed with both wisdom and fortune. Who can tell what parables it became for William and Sally? But a Brockdish boy, son of a servant of the overseers of the poor, child of a region that knew the human cost of enclosure, and sizar of Caius, might have seen in the daughter of a college cook, player of harpsichord and speaker of French, something of his own desire to have of "more than half a pair of shoes" and "gallop in a coach and six." In a romantic little joke was a metaphor of his own making good.

William galloped in a coach and six very many times in these early months of 1791. He was often on the move along the triangle that joined Brockdish, Cambridge and London. It is not easy to give a precise narrative of his transition from questionist at Cambridge to "Astronomer on board the *Daedalus*," despite twenty letters he wrote between 26 February and 17 August 1791. News of the expedition's need of an astronomer probably reached Cambridge before Christmas, 1790. In January, Samuel Vince and John Brinkley made Gooch's name known to Nevil Maskelyne, the Astronomer Royal. All then was haste and confusion till it was decided that the *Discovery* and *Chatham* would be followed

immediately by a supply ship. An astronomer would go with her and
have extra months to prepare. It gave time for Gooch's Cambridge
friends to lobby. Virtually the whole mathematical and astronomical
establishment of Cambridge was behind him. They wrote letters to admirals and lords, they forestalled Sir Joseph Bank's presumed right to
choose the "Experimental Gentlemen" of Pacific expeditions.

Maskelyne, an old rival of Banks, was easily persuaded of Gooch's
qualifications and began in April to prepare him for astronomical duties
which would not officially be his till a Board of Longitude meeting in
June.

In April Gooch came by "Fly" to London. Maskelyne set him to work
immediately on the instruments of his trade and on speedy and accurate
calculations of lunar angles and the time variations of Greenwich clocks.
Gooch's reports of his table talk with bishops and lords both heightened
his father's pride and quieted his mother's fears of the chills and dangers
that would come of making lunar observations on wet and windy decks.

These were delicious days, a spring novitiate in worldliness. Gooch
was polite, deferring, young. The first impulse of the worldly-wise
towards him was always to instruct and protect. So William Wales, long
experienced from Cook's voyages and master of mathematics at the navigational school at Christs Hospital advised him on the spending of his
astronomer's annuity of £400. Instead of sending it to his parents in
Brockdish, he should buy goods to trade with natives and make 5000%
on his investment. The mate and master of the *Daedalus*, surprised, they
said, that an astronomer was not old and wigged, would soon vow to be
his servants. Richard Hergest, his commander, would soon be his
brother, teach him French, educate him to shipboard life. Gooch spent
much money on the credit of his hopes, living in inns, catching the
"Fly," and moving his Cambridge belongings. Mothers of his Cambridge
friends fussed over him; and Mrs. Fearon thought he would be a bishop.

Gooch was not particularly well-prepared for his new venture. Second
Wrangler he might have been, but astronomer and navigator he was not.
He was accomplished at "fagging," however, and he had a shrewd eye
for vocational learning. He set about equipping himself with the means
to becoming an astronomer and navigator in foreign places. He bought a
fagger's library of useful knowledge. He knew little of the new world
that he would be soon surveying so he bought a *History of Spanish
America* and W. Guthrie's *New System of Modern Geography or a Geograph-
ical, Historical and Commercial Grammar*. His mother, already at work with
the Brockdish ladies making vests and breeches for antarctic waters and
shirts for tropical airs, might want assurances about his health. So he
bought John Elliot's *Medical Pocket Book* and William Buchan's *Domestic
Medicine*.

Gooch had little French and no Spanish and Italian. So he took a few distracted lessons from Señor Agostino Isola, who had prepared William Wordsworth for his travels abroad. Señor Isola was nicely described by a contemporary as "not a bowing man." His radical opinions isolated him in conservative Cambridge. Gooch came away from him with a clutch of dictionaries and grammars and a notion of how, alone in his cabin on a voyage around the world, he might improve his linguistic skills. He acquired *Don Quixote*, four volumes in English, six in French, another three in French and two in Italian. The old political radical sent him off to learn his languages from different translations of the *Devil on Two Sticks* as well. Perhaps the English edition of *Devil on Two Sticks* that he had was merely a translation of Alain Réné Le Sage's *Diable Boiteux*, the story of the very worldly education of Don Cleofas Leandro by the Devil Asmodeus. It could well have been William Combe's *Devil on Two Sticks in England.* The first two volumes appeared in March 1790 and the second two in January 1791. If it was, Señor Isola must have had some delight in thinking of the politically innocent Gooch getting a view from atop a London monument of an aristocratic class full of vanity and corruption and demoralized by the collapse of the old regime in Paris.

Gooch probably did not need to stand on a monument to see the world. His worldly education was rapid between January and June 1791. Patronage and trade were teaching him lessons not at all academic.

Gooch's pursuit of practical knowledge went further. On the advice of Samuel Vince, Brinkley and Maskelyne, he bought and borrowed from the Board of Longitude a small library that represented the state of astronomical and navigational research in 1791. Maskelyne's and Vince's own publications and tables were there, of course, as well as others by John Dollond, Giusepe Toaldo, Tobias Mayer, J. E. Bodes, De Moivre, William Bayly, William Wales. He took as many almanacs and calculating tables as were available at the time. His own eye was for the volumes that would give him directly and succinctly what he needed to know. Benjamin Martin, the British encyclopedist and popularist was there in *The Mariner's Mirror*. So was Haselden's *Seaman's Daily Assistant,* Wyld's and Gardner's *Practical Surveying*, Robertson's *Elements of Navigation.* They were all scientific and utilitarian, as scientific and utilitarian as William Paley and Robert Nelson. They were all of a tone with William Buchan's *Domestic Medicine*, a manual that deplored the veil of mystery over medicine. Buchan aimed to give the patient, through knowledge, the power of self diagnosis and cure. If there is a sense of what is shown of William Gooch in the volumes he had on his cabin shelves, it is that he had a scholastic confidence that most of life's problems could be "fagged" away. More than that. It showed a *mentalité* in which personal romance expressed in a social metaphor, religious devotion made sacrament in every daily act, science focussed on the resolution of practical problem, and social ambition tied to grasping the main chance were all of one piece.

William Gooch approached the major events of his life with pen in hand. He had scribbled notes to his parents through his Cambridge examinations. As he waited in the antechamber of the Board of Longitude at Admiralty Office on 12 June, he wrote again. The Board members had walked past him: Dr. Smith from Caius, Dr. Edward Waring (Lucasian Professor of Mathematics at Cambridge, who had examined him and Peacock), the Rev. D. Hornsby, (Savilian Professor of Astronomy at Oxford), John Pitt (Earl of Chatham and First Lord of the Admiralty), Rev. D. Shepherd (Plumian Professor of Astronomy at Cambridge), Philip Stephens and John Ibbetson (Secretaries of the Admiralty), and Sir Joseph Banks, "who give me a sly look as if he had been informed I was the person to be appointed." Sitting with Gooch and also waiting for a decision of the Board was Mr. Jesse Ramsden, "the first mathematical instrument maker in the world." Gooch heard Banks talk "very knowingly" with Ramsden about the universal theodolite that Gooch would soon take into the Pacific.

The Board finished the business of Gooch quickly and easily. On the Astronomer Royal's recommendation it resolved "that Mr. Gooch be appointed to proceed upon the service at a salary of £400 to commence this day, £200 to be paid in advance, and that half his salary be paid to him from time to time as it became due on his application for the same." They then reviewed the usual pile of eccentric proposals for discovering longitude. Perpetual motion machines, accurate sandglasses, water perambulators were always being thrust upon them. This day it was an instrument which, if fixed to the rudder, would prevent a ship overturning. They acknowledged its usefulness but said it did not contribute to their concern for longitude. They purchased Mr. Ramsden's "Azimuth and Altitude instrument" for 120 guineas. They gave the Astronomer Royal the task of checking new methods for making artificial horizons. They supported Maskelyne's preoccupying efforts to make scientific knowledge public. Maskelyne was not one for cosmological speculation. Theory did not interest him, but precise observation did. His Nautical Almanac was a notable contribution to the science of discovery and the practice of navigation. Ninety-thousand observations of moon and stars were put into navigators' hands. He went through twenty-five assistants in his forty-five years as Astronomer Royal. He bent their heads over calculations weeks and months on end and dismissed any one of them who compromised his independent calculations in any way. In an age still struggling to regulate time, he made transit observations, accurate to one-tenth of a second. In an age of patronage and entrepreneurial privacy of knowledge, he fought for clearer definition of the responsibilities of individuals and institutions supported by public moneys. No knowledge compiled at the Royal Observatory, he argued, should belong to an estate other than the king's. It should be shared. The papers of the Board and the Observatory, the Board decided, were to be sent to all the principal libraries and observatories of Europe.

There was no doubt that Maskelyne was bent on socializing Gooch to be a public man in his science. He secured his signed promise to return all instruments and publications loaned by the Observatory, "danger of the sea and other unavoidable accidents excepted." Even death was not counted as "unavoidable accident." For years Maskelyne chased every last page that was borrowed by the "Astronomer on Board the *Daedalus*." But there were private politics in this public science as well. One day Maskelyne was walking with Gooch on Blackheath together with his wife and daughter, Samuel Vince and John Brinkley, who was about to take up his appointment as Astronomer Royal in Dublin. Gooch reported Maskelyne's conversation to his father:

> Now I find people get a great notion of paying compliments and I have no notion of it at all and so d'ye see I hook 'em. The Irishmen thought it'd be a proper compliment to consult the English astronomer about the appointment of their new Irish one but, unluckily I don't think it proper to return the compliment by saying they couldn't be better supplied than from their own university and then they were all mad with me and themselves, too, except the Provost, and now some people are equally mad with themselves for having consulted me so much about the appointment of an astronomer for this expedition.

In this practical science of the astronomer, no language was more important to Gooch than that inscribed in his instruments. He might have found cribs on Spanish and French but being *bricoleur* in the science of the concrete things he must use was much more an alien experience. He took with him the prized products of the best instrument-makers of his day–Jesse Ramsden, Thomas Earnshaw, John Arnold, Edward Troughton, Edward Nairne, John Dollond. The personal imprint of these men on the instruments they made was and is so valued that virtually all the instruments Gooch took with him can now be traced to the observatories, museums and private collections that have preserved them. Learning the use of them was easy enough, although many a "young gentleman" who clung to ropes and stays on sloping decks while doing so might not have agreed. But Gooch was to be an "experimental gentleman." He must learn to read the science, the art, the very particular histories encapsulated in the artifacts he held in his hands.

Instrument-makers were artisans of precision. Jesse Ramsden had invented an "engine" that would make graduations of one four-thousandths of an inch. I despair of appreciating the poetics of such precision, let alone conveying the poetics of the science, art, and history texted into these artifacts that young William had to read. Edward Nairne, whose colored glass wedges, dipping needles, magnetic steel bars and pocket compasses Gooch took with him, described himself as maker of "philosophical apparatus." It was an apt description. I am embarrassed at my inability to catch the cosmology they display. They are truly "cargo" to me. I could not count the hours that I have pursued the text in Edward Troughton's "true flat glass" or Peter Dollond's achromatic lense, or John Arnold's helical spring in his pocket chronometer or Thomas Earnshaw's compensatory balance in his timekeeper so that I might read them with William Gooch's eyes. Yet I surely could not claim to present him in his Otherness unless I touched the significance he gave to the things that made him in his role as "Astronomer aboard the *Daedalus*."

I suspect these scientific things made by artisans, each brilliant in his different domain, were somehow "cargo" to William Gooch too. Despite his confidence in "fagging" himself to expertise in anything pertaining to knowledge, he seemed nervous in carrying out astronomical acts. Indeed the terror of his responsibility struck home even as the voyage began. Watches and clocks would dominate the rest of his short life. Winding them, calculating their losses and gains would take hours of his every day. When he arrived on board the *Daedalus*, the sign of his astronomer's office was his cabin, and he laid it out with all the sense of territoriality tidiness gives. He lovingly described to Goody Two-Shoes the contents of every drawer and shelf. Mr. Arnold's No. 14 and No. 46 and one of Mr. Earnshaw's timepieces were on the shelf before his eyes. Between Gravesend and Portsmouth the ship's cat dashed Mr. Earnshaw's watch to the floor. William Pitt, Gooch's servant, son of the Brockdish innkeeper, was sent posthaste by coach back to London with the news. Mr. Earnshaw, not amused, came posthaste down to Portsmouth with another, more expensive, watch. William Pitt lost his greatcoat in all this posthaste and almost missed the *Daedalus's* departure as well.

William Gooch was on board the *Daedalus* at Deptford in early July. His long voyage was begun. At its beginning as at its end it was full of Otherness. His energies at this time were spent in persuading his parents that the Otherness would not matter. He would mess with Hergest and Captain New "so I shall live in a family all the time I am in the ship." The "petty officers are willing to be my slaves." The mate will oblige him "in anything in his power." Hergest "in whose power it is to make time comfortable or not looks upon me as a brother." There would be savages in the Pacific but "the worst of savages is their immoderate propensity for stealing" and when they are caught at it they burst into laughter. He would fulfil his astronomer's duties at noon with the sun and at night with the moon but he would not have broken sleep and the master would likely do much of the observation. Besides, "I can never have such an opportunity of making myself known as by properly performing the office which I hope I may (without mistaken vanity) deem myself capable of." He had hoped that there would have been more of the £200 advance of his annuity to send them, but he was told he would make 5000% profit on the £20-30 worth of "baubles" he had bought. He has five dozen shoemaker's and butcher's knives, fifteen copper boilers, two dozen large scissors, and he would look for axes, chisels, hatchets. Two shillings worth would buy an otter's skin that would sell for $200-300 in China. There were other expenses–£50-60 cash that he must take with him, a watch he must buy. The poor boy from Brockdish would have to borrow £50 from Sally's parents, and £50 from the Bursar of Caius. But he had some scholarship from the London Fishmongers for six years that would give him the credit to borrow. He saw the need for a great variety of clothing for both "torrid zones" and cold climates, but the great cabin did not demand style. Blue and striped shirts would do. Indeed, he would take everything indiscriminately. The savages would not know the difference.

As Gooch coached his parents and Sally in the new proprieties of his life–the need to mute criticism when one moved among the great, the requirement to keep confidences–so he calmed their fears of these new and other worlds to which they were releasing him. He was trusting in character. By that he had something of a lien on Otherness, his trust made strange places more familiar.

Ambivalent Spaces

Familiarity on a ship was one thing, a strong stomach was another. They were not long out of Gravesend when Gooch was "obliged to heave a little ballast overboard" and Hergest was nursing his sea sickness with a little mulled wine and biscuit. A night ashore at Deal helped a little, but his poor sailoring raised a laugh when he scrambled into the boat bobbing beside the *Daedalus* with great difficulty.

Hergest drove the *Daedalus* towards Portsmouth against the wind, flying his navy pennant. It was his right, but a Whitby trader flying colors raised the curiosity of his Majesty's frigate *Vengeance*. *Vengeance* signalled *Daedalus* to heave-to. Hergest shouted their identity by trumpet and sailed on. *Vengeance* fired three muskets. Hergest said they were only shooting gulls and kept under way. *Vengeance* fired a ball through *Daeda-*

lus's rigging. It made a terrible rattling and snapping noise, said Gooch. "I had no idea that a ball made so much noise." Hergest bowed to circumstances and went by cutter to explain himself. For them all, it was the first real experience of their "governor" (as Captain New began to call him) at work.

At Portsmouth Hergest received his sealed orders. There had been rumors, hardly scotched by the Admiralty seals, of their destination. Gooch firmly believed it was to Chile, somewhere near Santiago. That was all right, he assured his parents, because the "total change of manners will make it seem like a new world." He was eager for strangeness.

Tide and wind would not come together at Portsmouth. The crew of the *Daedalus* made several aborted efforts to leave. Sally and Mrs. Smithson were there for each return to harbor save the last, and Gooch bemoaned that last chance. It was only late in London that he discovered, he wrote, "how strangely mistaken have I been in supposing Miss S. was indifferent to me." When he had told her then that they would see one another only one more time, she had burst into tears and run to her room. There he sat with her in the growing dark till she went to sleep. From London, to Gravesend, to Portsmouth they made one more time, till there was none.

From Portsmouth to Teneriffe Gooch experienced seas which he called rough but which the sailors, crawling around the deck, called moderate. Travellers' tales get little sympathy from other travellers. He would experience what rough might be at the Horn. He would understand then why sailors thought landsmen "milksops." He freely admitted that he could not do what they did in such conditions. But he did demand a little sympathy from more unknowing ears. The drinking water, he wrote, was as black as tea: one could not even see the bottom of the cup.

It is not from Gooch's hand that we learn of Hergest's violent trouble with his crew at Teneriffe. That comes from a note Sir Joseph Banks wrote himself. Banks might have heard of it from one of his correspondents on board Vancouver's *Discovery*, or from Captain New. When the *Daedalus's* voyage was over, Captain New made the circuit of those in London who had interests in the Pacific. There are notes of his conversations with Thomas Haweis who was about to begin his founding work of the Missionary Society. Missionaries would go to where the *Daedalus* had been–Tahiti and the Marquesas.

At Teneriffe Gooch recorded his first disagreement with Hergest. Significantly it concerned his first claim to independence as an astronomer. He wished to land to make some observations, but Hergest did not want to wear his cables in deep water. Hergest's brotherliness would prove to be irksome when he would brook no difference or criticism.

Rio De Janeiro was more rewarding. Gooch had the opportunity to play the astronomer in earnest. He unpacked his observatory and set up his instruments, he said, on an island in the bay. This was probably Ilha do Galeao, where there were shipyards at the time.

It was cloudy all the November days they were there, however. The weather moderated the excitement and novelty of making observations. A miscalculated meridian spoiled the memory of it, too, for it bedevilled him the rest of the voyage. They stayed at Rio De Janeiro three or four weeks, stocking water and supplies for the long run to Hawaii. Rio was proving to be an important stopover for British expansion in the Pacific. Convict vessels bound for Botany Bay, as packed with supplies as the *Daedalus*, would pause at Rio before crossing to the Cape of Good Hope and then navigating the long western passage to Australia. The *Pitt* was in harbor at the time of the *Daedalus's* arrival, although Gooch did not mention it. Sir Joseph Banks, who knew everything, reported that a convict on board the *Pitt* had repaired the micrometer screw on the astronomer's Troughton sextant. Alexander Davison, incidentally, had supplied the *Pitt* with £8406/19/8 worth of goods for a fee of £439/11/0. He had supplied seventeen other convict ships to this date with £79,032 worth of goods for a £4151 fee. Aboard the *Pitt* forty-seven men, women and children had died of smallpox and malignant fever even before reaching Rio. The 402 convicts were so crowded that their bodies were touching virtually all the time. They were, however, helping buy Mr. Davison's palatial house in St. James Square.

Rio was comfortably Stranger to Gooch. Portuguese and Catholics were sufficiently native to intrigue him in their Otherness. So he visited monasteries and libraries and gentlemen's houses. He accepted their difference with sufferance, although the hygiene of vermin-picking gentlemen, the cruelty of the slave market, the confinement of women and the authoritarian power of the Viceroy disturbed him. He spoke to friars in Latin and discovered that Cambridge Latin and Rio Latin were not quite the same. He was slightly scandalized at the precociousness of one of his women guests. He enjoyed Captain New's tricks on the foreigners. New had a bald pate like a tonsure. He claimed clerical privilege in the market, getting the best that was for sale. Gooch hosted a dinner for four local residents with what seems like gargantuan hospitality: two pork pies, two chicken pies, two loins of pork, two boiled chickens in soup, turkey, two large baked puddings, three to four dozen cream tarts—all ferried hot from the town bakery.

Hergest featured in another crisis for the *Daedalus's* crew at Rio. Walking in the town with young Tom, Captain New's son, Hergest had fondled children in a friendly way but offered some gesture to a woman that was misinterpreted. A crowd gathered angrily and stones were thrown. In retreating, Tom and Hergest were separated. Hergest rushed back to the *Daedalus* in a demented rage, thinking that Tom was hostage. He collected swords, pistols and muskets, ordered six men into a boat and went off to the assault. He could hardly explain it all in his anger. Then Tom appeared in a canoe. Hergest returned chagrined. Tom had simply run back a different way. So they all laughed at Hergest and laughed again. In an interesting revelation of what was already the subject of their conversations, Captain New said: "our Governor is so used to savages that he's dreaming he's among them already." Then they painted a picture of Hergest "storming the Brazils" with British courage, and fell about with amusement at it. New explained to the mystified Portuguese guard that they had a Don Quixote for a commander, and the guard gave an understanding smile. Gooch was about to add another sally but caught the mortified look in Hergest's eye and the emptiness of the "Governor's" laughter, and knew it was enough. "Who in the world," Gooch wrote of him, "could be more absurd thus to take armed men ashore when he knew he must not suffer them to fire, or if he did, be brought to a court of justice, but it was too comfortable with a great deal of his inconsistent conduct."

The *Daedalus*'s next stop was the Falklands. The ship nearly ran aground at Port Stevens. The crew had the eerie experience of creeping along the dangerous shore, seeing fires and hearing what they thought were voices. In the morning they discovered that the fires were of turf spontaneously set alight and the voices were the cries of sealions. They hunted geese and duck and sealions and fed themselves well. The killing of sealions was dangerous and barbarous. Franklin, the seaman, had done it before and exulted in it. Gooch fired one shot, discovered that he could hurt but could not kill, and withdrew. He could not cope with the sealions as they shielded their young and one another from the balls and spades. "I immediately hated myself for being an accomplice," he wrote.

Within a day of leaving the Falklands, 30 January, the weather turned bad. Gales from the north and west drove them nearly to 60°South and at times they were pushed back across the wind. They had experienced terrible seas before the Falklands. The deck railing had been snapped off. Water had tumbled down the companion-way and through a stern leak. The great cabin was at times awash. With the deadlights up, Gooch sat lashed in his chair in the dark, talking of schooldays with Mr. Pitt, playing "90's" or "blind O's" (probably a sort of noughts and crosses) on slates. Captain New, bruised by a fall and suffering gout, gave no cheer, as he predicted doom from moving cargo.

Now around the Horn it all happened again. Ten days of high seas and Gooch's admiration for the seamen grew. Ten days of waves "running wild and free" with little food save maggoty biscuit and the cook's hot chocolate was a double luxury out of Brazil. Then came the deliciousness of sunny breezes and silvery seas and sleeping languid and invalid all day. Off went the breeches and stockings, on went the linen jacket and trousers. Out came the "fagging" book for calculations. "As true as I am an astronomer 'tis just 2 O'clock!!! I will go to bed as you are rising," Gooch wrote to Goody Two-Shoes.

It is an ill wind that blows nobody good, and Hergest believed his wind had put them on a track on which no ship had run. Every day a man was at the mast looking for new land. The voyage of the hired transport on supply had become a voyage of discovery.

Six weeks of looking found nothing. This vast segment of the Pacific was as empty as it ever was, and the *Daedalus*'s track was as evanescent as any other ship's. 21 March came and there was an astronomical event, an eclipse of the sun. The astronomer seemed to get little joy out of it and merely bemoaned the ten digit calculations it required. The voyage had turned long and sour. Gooch's fag-book registered the boredom—pages of practiced gothic script and puzzles. In his journal he was forever counting the miles from home, and the months.

On 22 March the *Daedalus* sighted Fatuiva in the Marquesas and was soon sailing the passage between Hiva Oa and Tahuata. Vaitahu, the bay where it anchored, had been called "Madre De Dios" by the Spaniards in 1595 and "Resolution" in 1774 by Cook. The crew did not know that a Frenchman, Etienne Marchand, and an American, Josiah Roberts, had been there just a little time before. Had they known, they might have been a little more nervous of the native disorder. Marchand's visit was characteristic of the Gallic innocence of early French Pacific voyaging, not at all like the gross intrusion of empire at a later date. He scrupled taking possession of the islands, even in the name of his new revolution. In his eyes the islands were already possessed by the free spirits of the natives. The visit by Josiah Roberts, on the other hand, was full of cruelty and murder. He had established camp at Vaitahu to assemble a pre-fabricated yacht meant to make his northwest trading easier. When the islanders showed resentment at his appropriations, he killed them indiscriminately.

In his journal, Gooch wrote that the natives he saw flinching at the sight of a musket did so because one of Cook's marines had killed the thief of a penny nail with a single shot eighteen years before. But they had been bloodied more recently and more copiously than that. Gooch's encounter with them had no history that he could see. He was blind except for his own imaginings about who they might be and how they might act. It was a dangerous innocence, a Present that had no Past. 22 March was the night of the fire and the broken cable. Gooch scrupled whether to tell his parents about the danger the ship had been in, but he gave them some account. He also assured them it could never happen again. What would the crew have done had the fire got out of hand, he asked. They would simply have sailed their longboat to "Otaheite," where they knew Captain Bligh would be collecting breadfruit again in the *Providence*. The Present with natives might have no Past, but a once unknown ocean was now being made familiar and secure by these acts of empire.

After Tahuata, the *Daedalus*'s natural direction to Hawaii was north. She immediately came upon the northern or windward Marquesas. Hergest thought he had made his discovery. They approached each island, gave it a name, surveyed and mapped it, made pleasant contact and exchange with the large numbers of canoes that made friendly gestures. Gooch's fag-book was orgiastic with calculations. He would be ready to dazzle Dr. Maskelyne. Indeed, Gooch's charts of what Vancouver later called "Hergest's Islands" were his only contribution to science. It was a small and brief one. Maskelyne was to be fairly dismissive of the work Gooch had done in the Atlantic as nothing new, and by the time he got Gooch's maps of "Hergest's Islands" there was the embarrassment that they were not "Hergest's" at all, but "Joseph Ingraham's," an American, who had called them "Washington Islands." The *Daedalus* had not made History after all. They were not "first," and Gooch's maps were, for that reason, uninteresting.

Vancouver, perhaps because he wanted some memorial for his friend Hergest, was not willing to concede that the revolutionary Americans were "first." "Hergest's Islands," he understood could actually be seen on a clear day from a high point in the southern Marquesas, so really they were part of the original Spanish discovery or even that of Captain Cook, who put the Marquesas accurately on the map. New Englanders were more tenacious of their past, however. Several times they triumphantly proved in the Massachusetts Historical Society journal that Joseph Ingraham was "first." The French as usual made History in their own way. Come the days of their empire, they simply erected a stone and a plaque on Nukuhiva which announced that Etienne Marchand was "first." It is still there.

Hergest's appetite for discovery had been whetted. He sailed north-northwest. He should have pointed more closely into the north-northeast winds. His easy north-northwest tack would mean the *Daedalus* would get to the lee of the Hawaiian Islands and be forced to beat back to them. This would delay her already late arrival. Vancouver would be gone. Gooch and his "Governor" fell out again over the propriety of this. Hergest, doomed to traverse the Pacific whatever happened, had not much to lose by being late. Gooch was eager for his real work to begin and was desperately weary of the *Daedalus*.

Virtually all Gooch's days were now filled with translating his calculations into maps of the *Daedalus*'s new found islands. Confined to the great cabin, he now lost another friend and felt his good fortune was running out. Captain New at the beginning of their voyage had presented him with a spaniel puppy. "Tio" they had called him. *Taio* was the Tahitian word for 'friend'. Along with "taboo," "tayo" had become one of the first Polynesian words to cross the Polynesian/European boundary. They were misappropriated words, of course, and never meant, in the episodes of contact, what the islanders meant of them. Tio, the spaniel, had had the run of the *Daedalus*, chasing waves, celebrating fishing successes, balancing precariously between the railings. He and Bot, Hergest's dog, had caused pandemonium among the Marquesans who had no dogs. Dogs had become extinct in their islands. Tio had clearly been an affectionate companion for Gooch. Captain New had been shrewd in his gift-giving. Somewhere between the Marquesas and Hawaii Tio disappeared. He had fallen overboard unnoticed. By that Gooch's voyage had become more sour still.

The *Daedalus* anchored at Kealakekua on the island of Hawaii on 28 April. Vancouver had sailed, only ten days before, according to the "childish lies" of an Hawaiian, much earlier–on 4 March–according to Vancouver's waiting letter.

The *Prince William Henry*, trading on the northwest coast under Captain Evans, was at Kealakekua. She was at first alarmed at the appearance of the *Daedalus*, thinking she might be the *Bounty* with its mutineers. Gooch took advantage of the *Prince William Henry's* presence to send a packet of letters to his parents on the probability that the trader would soon meet up with some ship returning to England. It was to be Gooch's last letter to them. It was short, hearty and embarrassed. He had not written to them since Rio. He could not say it to them but his depressions had made him lethargic:

> God almighty bless you both and grant us all a happy meeting at the earliest period we can hope for (which is toward Autumn 1794) but perhaps a year longer. Think not this conciseness (if you should receive this packet) a breach of filial duty, but believe that I am and ever will remain your dutiful and affectionate son.

The *Prince William Henry* was experiencing difficulty with the Hawaiians. She only wanted water and supplies, but the Hawaiians wanted "trade." She only wanted cheap things, for which there was no reason to pay the muskets and weapons the Hawaiians wanted. So the Hawaiians dawdled with the watering, lost the casks, and stole. There was no profit in that kind of frustration. So on 2 May the *Prince William Henry* pulled anchor and it was the *Daedalus's* turn to be teased.

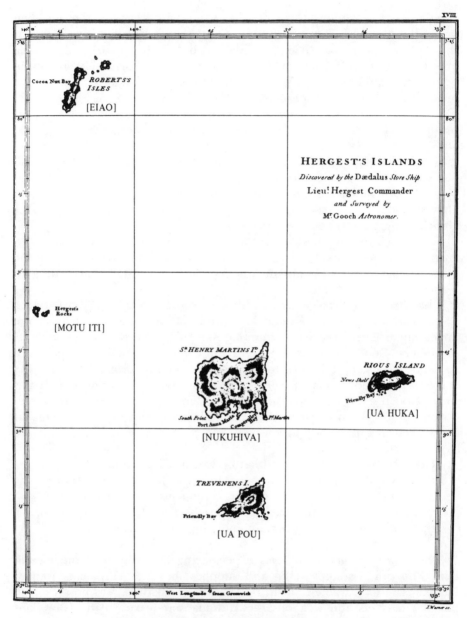

FIGURE 7: "HERGEST'S ISLANDS" WITH MARQUESAN NAMES IMPOSED
(from George Vancouver, *A VOYAGE OF DISCOVERY*, 1798).

Double Entendre

Teasing was a sign of the *double entendre* that was now beginning to contextualize Gooch's life. In the place where Captain Cook had been killed and the "Governor" of the *Daedalus* had, as a young man, played out his view of how to deal with savages in extravagant charade, it was unlikely that Hergest would suffer teasing easily. He seemed not to have gone ashore at Kealakekua. Probably it would have been dangerous, and certainly he was unlikely to cope well with the ambivalences of sitting beside those whom he had so desperately tried to kill. So he managed from a distance. He was in the hands of the "Rascal Merchant's" men to get supplies for his ship: he was in the hands of an inexperienced boy, William Gooch, to be the diplomat with "King" Kamehameha. He was in the hands of Kualelo ("Towerero" or "Charles," an Hawaiian whom Vancouver had brought back to Hawaii) to mediate between the native Hawaiians and the stranger ship. The tensions in him grew and disturbed his relations with all around him. The ambiguities of this marginal space mounted.

Kualelo had appeared as soon as the *Daedalus* anchored. He was full of fantastic stories. He fought for Kaiana and Kamehameha, he said, in their battle for Hawaii. He had killed twenty-two men in a day and had been rewarded with land by chiefs and priests. He was liberated of "taboos." His capital was his familiarity with two cultures. But he was also *poseur* to both and neither knew what he really understood of the other. Kualeolo claimed to have Vancouver's letter. However it was actually in the possession of Kamehameha and someone would have to go to him to get it. While Hergest hesitated as to who this would be, Gooch forestalled his decision and joined Kualelo on his canoe. It should have been a short trip to Kamehameha's residence on the point of Kealakekua Bay, but Kualelo, eager to show his importance, took off for two hours down the coast to show Gooch his land. There he played the chief, beating off with a stick the 700-800 commoners who crowded around to see the young Stranger. It was dark when they returned to Kealakekua, their canoe lighted by torches. Along the shore men with more torches followed their course.

Kualelo and Gooch had picked up the mate of the *Prince William Henry*, Mr. Wick, on the way. Together they went to Kamehameha in his "palace." The chief was very welcoming. He ordered a pig for their meal, inquired after King George's health and asked whether the British monarch was as stout as he. He requested Mr. Wick to entertain them with "military exercises" with a musket. Mr. Gooch could not do so, because he was not a military man, but he dandled Kamehameha's son, "King George," on his knee. The whole party ate the pork, with one knife between them. When Kamehameha drank, Kualelo pushed Gooch's head to the ground. Drinking was a high chiefly act that none might see. Gooch and Wick slept that night in the "King's" sleeping house which was also the storage for twenty-two muskets. They had processed to the sleeping-house together, Kamehameha with musket in hand, Gooch carrying the cartridges. They slept–"Queen," "King," Gooch, and Wick– side by side. Or so Gooch would have slept, had not the guard of ten at the entrance to the house played the drum all night.

During the evening Hergest sent an admonishing letter to Gooch. Gooch wrote that he intended to keep the letter, no doubt as evidence of Hergest's extravagances, should his reputation later be impeached. Hergest's letter, however, has not survived. The next morning, back on the *Daedalus*, bruised and hurt by Hergest's attitude, Gooch wrote his reply, in "Greek."

The *Daedalus* remained nine or ten days at Kealakekua, till 6 or 7 May. Neither Kaiana's or Kamehameha's people could be persuaded to complete the watering. The ship's gig was stolen and retrieved after violent threats. One-hundred-and-six pigs were purchased at one four- teen-inch *toa* ('iron tool') each. Davison's men were "trading" with the stores he had secreted on board. Kualelo was in a sulk because he had heard unkind things said about him and because Hergest refused his request to be taken to Maui. He showed his chagrin by jumping out the great cabin window without saying goodbye. During those days a large double canoe approached the *Daedalus*. The canoe was apparently captained by a woman. She asked for muskets and would only go away when weapons were threateningly pointed at her. In the end, Hergest up-anchored and made for Waimea.

These were uncomfortable days for Gooch. A great cabin in which communication is by "Greek" letters is a place divided. He did not go ashore again. He managed his affairs with gifts. He left packets of letters with Kaiana to post by the next ship and gave him some red baize. There was no sign of 5000% profit out of his investments. He ruminated that the taboo-bound Hawaiians were as "priest-ridden as catholics" and pitied their subjection to the arbitrary power of "rascals." He watched from the ship's railing as the Hawaiians caught sharks in the waters around the ship. Each day, for the last three days that they were in Kealakekua, the Hawaiians searched for and caught sharks, three and four in a day. Sometimes when two fished for the same shark, one would catch it by the tail. "Sharks, sharks" were the last notes he wrote.

Gooch could no more see what the Hawaiians did when they caught sharks than he could see the Hawaiian culture that contexted this "priest-ridden" society. He, no doubt, was as shrewd as anybody in reading human universals of greed and vanity, anger and pride, tender- ness and guile. What he could not read was the History they made of the events in which they were conjoined with him. It would be fraud of me–who has gone so far in making my own History of the death of William Gooch–to suggest that I can read with much greater assurance than Gooch the *double entendre* of these events. But since the voyage is near its end, let me begin to make my readings.

The same dialectic of circumstance and structure that took Gooch from Brockdish to Kealakekua Bay was taking Koi and his killers to Waimea. Our hindsighted knowledge of what happened makes a drama of their coming together on 12 May from two sides of the globe. It is the irony of our History that we see what they could never see, the consequences of every accident and option that drove them to their meeting. For us even chance makes sense because it evolved into something that happened in a particular way at a particular time. And while we cannot count the structural conditions of culture and society that limit the play of chance, we make sense of personality, of class, of mythic perceptions and weave our understanding of their inevitability to our hindsighted sureness that something happened very particularly. By that we have a story. By that we have a History.

If I could have done for Koi, Kapaleaiuku and Kuaniu, the men who killed him, what I have done for Gooch, I might have written well-rounded History. But I cannot offer my half guesses about them as something surer.

I want to say that since the only Past that remains is an after-meditation, the structures we see are always History, always meanings made. We never have the assurance that these meanings were predictive determinants of events still to come. We only have interpretation of what has gone before. But we know that these constructed meanings belong to public systems and, because of that, are out of time. They wrap particular events around.

I cannot tell, for example, whether Kamehameha, when he met Gooch, had already experienced or was anticipating the great mythic moment of his life, had he sacrificed or was he about to sacrifice Keoua, his rival for Hawaiian kingship? We do not know the precise time of that event, any more than we know whether it was Keoua's naivete and Kamehameha's treacherous guile that ruled the moment or some self-conscious playing out of mythic proprieties on their parts. We do know that by the sacrifice Kamehameha's violent usurping power was transformed into legitimate, kingly authority–ritually, mythically and historically. The meanings made wrapped the particularities of naivete and guile around and took them out of time.

"Sharks, sharks" wrote a lethargic, despondent Gooch. He could not know that sharks and gods and strangers and chiefs had "sparkling eyes." He could not know the metonymies Hawaiians made of sharks as gods and chiefs and strangers. He could not know the meanings that would enclose his inexperience, Hergest's imprudence, Hawaiian greed for weapons–and put them out of time.

Hergest disobeyed the orders that Vancouver left for him at Hawaii. By those orders, he was to sail to Waikiki then to Nootka. He sailed to Waimea instead. Vancouver excused him later by presuming that he was probably making for Nootka the more quickly. But Hergest's sense of History was upon him. He was making a tour of his past. As soon as he got to Waimea, he had acceded to the request of the old Hawaiian who came aboard to take him back to Kauai after their stay at Waimea. Hergest was in no haste for Nootka. He would go to Kauai and by that touch at all the places he had been with Cook.

Limits to Circumstance

The *Daedalus* arrived off Waimea on the afternoon of 7 May–there are some differences about the date in varying accounts, but that would be more a problem for admiralty paymasters calculating settlements they owed the dead than for us. Hergest did not intend to anchor at Waimea, only to barter with canoes at a distance from the shore. He did not intend to anchor, Vancouver reported, because he "considered the inhabitants of that neighbourhood to be the most savage and deceitful of any amongst those islands." Whether Hergest sustained this prejudice from his first visit fourteen years earlier or whether he had learned something at Kealakekua we cannot say. Certainly his prejudice inflated the error of his subsequent imprudence.

The calm of the evening of 7 May allowed currents to take their effect on the *Daedalus*. The crew were forced to make sail for sea and, for three days, could not make their way back. On the afternoon of 11 May they returned to Waimea. Hergest set the cutter at the stern to trade with canoes there.

Behind, on the *Daedalus*, the crew began to "trade" for "artificial curiousities." Exchange in the cutter stopped. Hergest flew into a rage with both the crew and the Hawaiians. He shoved the Hawaiians overboard and ordered the mate, Mr. Neal, to form a crew for the cutter, row ashore for water, and take no arms. Neal refused to obey. So Hergest chose a crew himself, looked to Gooch to come with him and went off. Captain New surreptitiously put some muskets in the bottom of the cutter.

The men in the cutter had time enough to see where they were going as they rowed the three miles to shore. They steered for the "remarkable and romantic bluffhead," that the *Resolution* had described. Before them in the water, across the front of the beach, were shoals of black rock, a passage-way clear between them. On their left high on Keanaloa, the northern or eastern bluff that dominated the stream, was the temple

Puu-o-Mahuka. Its *anu'u* ('high tower') was conspicuous and the wooden houses of its sanctuary could be seen. They might have seen as well the fishermen's lookout from which the fishing canoes were directed to their shoals. Kuala and Kaneaukai were the fish gods of the bay. There was hardly a rock in the sea that did not have a name and, with the name, a history. On their right, below the northern or eastern bluff (Kalua hole) were clusters of houses and canoes. There were other *heiau* and shrines on the bluffs to be seen as well.

Waimea ('reddish waters') was a river of floods, a composite of three streams. In 1792 the detritus had not raised the beach as high as it is today. The men could take their cutter almost to the fork of the rivers between the bluffs and beach it beside the small delta the floods had already made. They beached it to the southern or western side of the bay.

It was what they could not see, one has to suppose, that mattered. They could not see the season or the time in which they came. They could not see the space they entered upon. They could not see the History that was about to wrap their lives around. Kahekili, high chief of Maui, mortal enemy of Kamehameha, had finally got Oahu in his power and had ruled it for ten years through his son, Kalanikapule. Waimea itself was priestly land, mythically associated with the priest Kaopulupulu who had thwarted Kahekili's hegemony and warned of its consequences. But Waimea was also on the edge of Waialua, a district of rebellion for Kahekili. In Waialua's history was a bitter story of broken resistance to Kahekili's usurping power. Waimea, with Waialua, was the back blocks to Waikiki. Waimea was a marginal space of power and authority. In token of its marginality, Kahekili had left Koi at Waimea to guard the weak spot of Oahu while Kahekili battled Kamehameha on Maui and Hawaii.

In those wars with Kamehameha, Kahekili had learned that the face of battle had changed with Kamehameha's acquisition of swords, knives, muskets, even cannon and European ships. Kahekili had lost the sea battle of Kepuwahaulu. In 1791 his soldiers were routed on Maui itself by Kamehameha's cannons. Getting guns was a primary need, recruiting European beachcombers to mediate the technology a close second. Sandalwood, a prize that would force European captains to trade guns, was only just being discovered. James Coleman, whom we met at Vancouver's trial and execution of Gooch's alleged killers, was one of the first sailors to be left by captains to organize the sandalwood trade. Kahekili had made life more attractive to Coleman and he became an armorer in residence at Waikiki. Safe ports for refurbishing during the winter on the northwest coast were a second prize for traders. Beachcombers could manage safe ports and by that buy guns for their chiefs.

A

B

FIGURE 8: (A) WILLIAM ELLIS'S DELICATE WATERCOLOR OF WAIMEA
(reversed for engraving; from the Carter Collection, Bishop Museum).
(B) PHOTOGRAPH OF WAIMEA LOOKING TOWARDS THE FORKED STREAM.
(Hergest and Gooch walked towards the central bluff. The *heiau*
of *Pu'u o Mahuka* stood on the left bluff. The Hawaiian houses
Were located to the right and the *Daedalus's* cutter was beached
to the forward left, out of the photograph.)

So the disorder of marginal places had a double advantage for Hawaiians. Arms could be stolen, boats cut off and the danger would drive the Europeans to the managed security of Waikiki or Lahaina or Kealakekua. As the Hawaiians understood it in their histories of the death of Gooch, the chiefs of Oahu–Kahekili and his governor–had instructed the lesser chiefs in quiet places to gather weapons in whatever way they could. As Kahekili and his governors understood it in their histories of the death of Gooch, these quiet, out-of-the-way places were full of bands of wild men whose behavior they could not guarantee.

When I say that the face of battle was changed by European weapons, I only mean that the mask of battle was changed. What battle represented, what meanings were made of it, was hardly transformed at all. Kahekili was *pahupu*, 'cut-in-two'. Kahekili was a familiar of the god of thunder, Kanekehili, and, like any child born with a black birthmark on one side of the body, was chosen by Kanehekili. Kanehekili killed those who cursed and abused him and those who conspired against him by lightning and thunder. All over the Polynesian Pacific the European Strangers came in the lightning and thunder of their arms. All over the Pacific, and in Hawaii, there was an easy appropriation of the myths of thunder to the Strangers. There was an easy sacramentalizing of their symbols of power to signs of divine presence. The battle had not changed at all.

Koi was *pahupu*, too. He was one of Kahekili's cohort of chiefly soldiers and a sacrificing priest of the *heiau* of Kapokea at Waihe'e on Maui as well. Waihe'e ('squid waters') was an appropriate place of origin for a man as thoroughly inked as Koi: the falls of the river at Waimea were called Waihe'e also. Koi was one of Kahekili's commanders who had experienced the defeat at the sea battle of Kepuwahaulu. He knew the value and meaning of thunder. He had ownership of the great sacrifice *heiau* of Puu-o-Mahuka. He probably lived in Kohokuwelowelo, the fearsome dwelling place of the *kahuna* ('priests'). We have to think that it was he who came out to the *Daedalus* to bargain for arms, that it was he whom Hergest pushed overboard, that it was he who, some of the crew said angrily, pursued the cutter to the shore.

When the cutter landed, four crew remained aboard it. Hawaiians rolled the casks to the nearest fresh water at the base of the southern or western bluff. Manuel stayed there supervising the watering. Hergest, Gooch and Franklin crossed the river and walked up inland along the bank. They had not gone far when Hergest sent Franklin back with instructions about the bunging of the casks. They must have seen, at about the same time, the alarm among the Hawaiians as women ran from the houses and men moved their canoes inland. When Franklin reached Manuel, he saw a "blackfellow" running down the hill with a large knife. They decided to move towards the boat. The man with the

knife began to harangue the Hawaiians and cry "Taboo! Taboo!"
Whether it was the watering that was *kapu* or their return to the boat,
we cannot say. Franklin heard Manuel cry out but was immediately
himself seized about the waist. Perhaps that was a sign that the Hawaiians were trying to capture another beachcomber. He broke free and
charged through them to the boat. Meanwhile, a crowd of Hawaiians
had come down from the opposite bluff behind them and cut off
Hergest and Gooch. Hawaiian histories say that Gooch was killed first,
stabbed through the chest with a spear. Hergest was stunned and then
killed with a stone. Franklin's last sight of them suggested that Gooch
was already dead and his body was being dragged away. Hergest was in
the middle of a cluster of Hawaiians.

After-Meditation

So William Gooch was dead. What killed him? His going to Cambridge?
His utilitarian spirit and his false sense of confidence in easily controlling
his life? The intrusion of empire on native peoples? The greed for profit
in the purchase of "artificial curiousities"? The ambivalent symbols of a
ship part-navy, part-trade? The personal history of an erratic Hergest?
The peaks and troughs of a volatile friendship? The ambiguities of
Waimea, a beach between Native and Stranger, a beach in Hawaiian
polity? The politics of chiefs? The accidents of misconstrued signs?

The Hawaiians thought Gooch was killed because he had "sparkling
eyes," because he was a god, Lonoikouali'i. Not Lono, he had died at
Kealakekua in the person of Captain Cook. Lonoikouali'i belonged to
Oahu and was worshipped there. Lonoikouali'i had come from the sea
with Oahu's migrative chief, Lonoikamakahiki. Lonoikamakahiki had
come from a far-place, Kahiki. They knew Gooch was a god, because
when he was dead and sacrificed, the thunder from the sea did not hurt
them. No doubt he would come again, as he had come before, and the
chiefs would eat his sparkling eyes again. So they parcelled up his body
among the chiefs and archived his bones in a *heiau*–Mokuleia they
said–so that History could be made over again in every sacrifice.

Where will we put that History in our understanding of why Gooch
was killed?

There is one more after-meditation. Old William Gooch left some
notes in the bundle of papers that were the relics of his son's life.

Early Friday January 24 1794. I dreamed my son was arrived at
Brockdish alive and well. I conversed with him in dream. He said
he must go again. I charged him to take care of himself. He
promised not to venture into danger. We were both happy at his

going and confident of his future safety. I had a melancholy wakening.

March 4 1794. I dreamed my son escaped being massacred and arrived home. I asked him how far it might be that Mr. Hergest and himself walked beyond the watering place when the savages first attacked them. I do not remember his answer or whether he made one.

Where will we put that?

5

REFLECTIONS

Much of the work I have done as an historian has been done in the Children's Mission Library, Honolulu, Hawaii. The library, small and open to the trade winds, lies among coconut palms in the mission cemetery. When the microfilm reader has become too overpowering, or when there has seemed more dust than light in the archives, I have walked in the cemetery among the gravestones.

My historical work has always concerned Natives and Strangers in the Pacific: Natives, spread through all the Pacific on their myriad islands; Strangers come to the Pacific from distant places for reasons of discovery or empire or trade or religion. On a world scale (or snob rating), the events that concern me are not large, but their mystery is larger than my understanding, so I am happier by far to live by the hopes of my puzzlements than by the vanity of their importance.

The cemetery in Honolulu is a cemetery of Strangers mostly. The bones of missionaries are archived in their graves while their papers are archived in the library. The bones and papers of the "People of Old," the Natives, are less handily catalogued. The epitaphs on the Strangers' gravestones make edifying reading. They search out metaphors that express confidence and victory, self-sacrifice and faith. Gravestones are rhetorical documents. It is a brave man who carves his irony or his doubts or his in-between character in stone.

There are several graves, however, that have caught my attention. One is the grave of Willie Nevins Alexander. I know Willie Nevins well. He was the infant son of a missionary in the Marquesas Islands. He was born on Nukuhiva in the Marquesas in 1834 and died in Lahaina in Hawaii in 1835, living only one-year, two-months and fifteen-days. The Marquesans, for the brief time that they knew him called him *Hape* ('Upside-Down'). "Kaoha, Hape!," they used to call out as they passed by the thatched, closed mission hut where he was born. 'Upside-Down' was not a bad name for a Stranger born on a Polynesian beach. Stranger and Native both, but in-between, upside-down.

There is another gravestone that has caught my eye. It stands between an epitaph that exhorts us to bear one another's burdens and one whose assurance is manifest: "Behold I have graven thee on the palms of my hands." Between these two there is one that reads simply: "Sister Kate, She hath done what she could." There is not much rhetoric in that. I like it. I think that I would like an epitaph on my grave that would read: "*Hape*, Upside-Down, In-Between. He did what he could." It suits my sense of History.

A sense of History is difficult to describe, and, as I have long discovered, impossible to prescribe. That writer of epigrams to soothe as well as to stir souls, Thomas à Kempis, wrote that he would rather feel compunction of the heart than know how to define it. It was his caution to neophytes in the spiritual life against too much theoretical reflection. And Hilaire Belloc, a gruffer type of spiritualist, had a similar message:

> The water beetle glides upon the water's face
> With ease, celerity and grace.
> But if it stopped to think
> Of how it did it, it would sink.

Most historians would take comfort from such warnings. They would rather write history than know how to define it, and they have a suspicion that too much thinking leads to sinking.

Indeed this was the point made rather forcibly to me by one of my teachers of history when I went to say goodbye to him as I left to do my doctoral studies in anthropology at Harvard University. "Dening," he said, "I have to say that I think that this is the end of your academic career." He had a prejudice against American education, but it was the anthropology that stuck in his craw. Anthropology offended him. It relativized proper objects of study. Natives in anthropology were as revealing of human nature as Strangers, and that was an affront to somebody who thought human nature was enshrined in Adam Smith. Indeed, there was something improper in doing what I wanted to do–the anthropology of Strangers as well as Natives. Culture in his view had something of the old school tie: Strangers' culture did not need an anthropology. Worst of all, in anthropology, nothing commonsensical could be taken for granted, not politics, not religion, not even economics. In anthropology, the proper stance before the infinite variety of human experience is a reflective one. There is not much Otherness, or reflection, to be found in common sense.

Doing anthropology at Harvard was not, as it happened, the end of my academic career. I have the satisfaction of sitting as an anthropologist in a chair of history. That is not to say that I have never felt uncomfortable in that chair. I have felt myself, and sometimes have been made to feel, upside-down, in-between.

I do not think it has been by accident that my major work has been about islands and beaches. I have been lured like a moth to the lamp by problems about boundaries and the way boundaries are made and crossed–boundaries between disciplines, boundaries between and within institutions, boundaries of culture and creed and color. I suppose I have gone to Pacific islands and ships and mission-stations and outposts of empire because there distinctions are displayed almost in caricature–between civilized and uncivilized, between the exploited and their oppressors, between the converted and the unconverted. And I suppose I have had an inordinate interest in the beachcombers of life, the in-between people. If you want my ultimate liberal philosophy to be revealed, let me say that I think it is the human condition to be in-between. Against the social pressure to be divided by role or sex, class or institution, ideology or culture, the actual experience of human beings is of process and invention, of accommodating what is given to the circumstances of interpretation. If the actual experience of human beings is of both order and change, of surrender to the definitions, reifications and divisions of society as well as resistance to them, then it is the burden of historians to describe what actually happened and of anthropologists to display this dialectic of human culture.

I take my historical task to be to describe what *actually* happened in the past. I call that ethnography. I am a little frightened by those who claim to describe what *really* happened. They have successively grabbed this or that bit of the human anatomy and environment as their own and made Frankenstein monsters of their models.

I do ethnographic history. I do not see that as twee–history with the politics left out, a trivial pursuit of morris dancing and the like. It begins with the most difficult thing of all to see: the experience of past actors as they experienced it, and not that experience as we in hindsight experience it for them.

"People are as they express themselves to be." So Karl Marx wrote. The only way to discover who people actually are is through their expressions, through their symbolic systems. This is not the place to give a lesson on ethnographic history. So let me say baldly that ethnography takes an historian to the systematic and public expression of who people are–their rituals, their myths, their symbolic environments.

Of all the systems that are expressive of who a people are, the sharpest and clearest is their historical consciousness. History belongs to us all, History is us all, in many different ways. And for all the different occasions in which we use History we have a different sense of it. Because we use it so differently, there is little point in claiming empire over one particular use. Our sense of History is embedded in our different usage. Our different usage is what History is, not what I or you say History should be.

We have different histories for different occasions. Perhaps this seems an obvious point, but for me it has been liberating, a discovery. I find our human ingenuity in reading words and occasions so variously comforting. Our readings are not anarchic. They are ordered. They have a poetic. We present ourselves by expressing a significant past.

Variation in the forms and the readings of those expressions do not detract from the fact that they are significant. We know who we are in our varied ways of History making.

Consider my introduction to this reflection, my story of Hape and Sister Kate. It was a story of part of my past. Was it History? Of course it was. It gave meaning to past events and occasions. It was crafted very much to my purposes. I have no real control over what it meant to you. What it meant to you is influenced by many things, by your expectancies of what I should be writing, by the strangeness of my vocabulary, by the peaks and troughs of your attention, by our changing relationship as you read. I know the meaning I intended my story to convey to you. It was not to inform you about missionary cemeteries in the Pacific. My purposes were to leave in your mind a sense of my cross-cultural interests in Native and Stranger, and a sense of my own feeling that the History I make is slightly disturbing to others, upside-down, in-between. I sculpted the story—in the economy of my words, in the rhythm of my phrases, in its tone and images. My story is fiction in that sense, like my story of the death of William Gooch. It is as effective a vehicle of my meanings as I can make it. My story is also a gift to you without strings, for you to enlarge it, make it relevant to your interests in whatever way you will. But I clearly hope that all of what I will have to say will become encapsulated in that story, that the story, with all the complex overtones of how and where you read it, will become a sort of "memory palace" for all the complex things I want to say about making History.

What I do here so self-consciously we all do unreflectively every day of our lives. In gossip, in nostalgic memories, in family anecdote, in toasts and speeches, in anniversary ceremonies, in *rites de passage*, in symbolic actions, we are always making History by crafted stories. We live by and in our crafted stories. Our social and cultural life is a theatre in which we display both ourselves and a significant past. And the meaning of our stories is us, in our roles, in our relationship, in the structures of our society, in the systems of our culture. We do it so often and so constantly that we can hardly see the art and science of our "memory palaces" for the making of them. So when I make History, I like to make History of people making History, because that is where they reveal themselves.

I know that I have already gone too far. For many historians we have "stopped to think," and sunk. While we might be thought to display ourselves in our varied presentations of the past, "academic history," some historians would say, is not like that. Discipline makes "history" different, takes away its poetic, gives assurance that the Past and History are the same. No, it does not. Discipline only makes the rules of our reading explicit. Discipline only makes our poetic self-conscious. There is no privilege for disciplined, or academic, history. It has its anthropology like all the rest.

The true privilege of all histories, disciplined and undisciplined, is that they each offer a liminal moment. They offer a "retreat." In-between Past and Present, in-between simulation and invention, in-between conserving and creating, histories are always metonymies of culture in process. In histories we know ourselves as limited by our given experience and liberated by our contrivance. Ultimately, I think that is History's Anthropology.

NOTES

Making History

My reconstruction of the histories that were made of the deaths of Hergest, Gooch and Manuel comes mostly from the reports of various members of Vancouver's expedition. Vancouver (1798 2:85, 1984 2:776) quotes Captain New's logs, and all the rest (Menzies 1923; Bell 1929-30; Howett 1789; Manby 1929) claimed insider's knowledge to the extent that they had seen New's log or spoken with the crew of the *Daedalus.* Young Tom New revealed–but had long enough been silent to show the significance he gave it–that the *Daedalus's* crew had bargained for Hawaiian artifacts. David Turner, the Norfolk antiquarian who collected Gooch's "Letters and Memoranda," added a letter of Tom Dobson to his father, a wine merchant in Vauxhall. It is the only extant account of a near witness. William Gooch's own father–never reconciled to his son's death, and eager to bring the blame of it home to Hergest–wrote bitterly to William Broughton, who was about to return to the Pacific. Broughton wrote a reply sensitive to the old man's grief and saying that he thought Hergest's actions were inexplicable, but that command was a hard thing. Old William Gooch kept his letter. Later visitors to Hawaii recorded the later ironies of the story (Byron 1826; Bloxham 1926; Iselin n.d.:69).

The Hawaiian accounts all flow out of the Lahainaluna Mission School's history-making. Missionary historians quote roughly the same accounts with different detail from their different informants (Dibble 1909:33; Bingham 1848:42; Jarves 1872:73). Fornander (1869:246ff.) is the richest and most reflective, making his own history to suit the political moments of 19th century Hawaii. Kamakau (1961:162ff.) and Ka Mooolelo Hawaii (1984:181-183) are the reports nearest to what the Lahainaluna oral record had been.

William Ellis's watercolor of Waimea is our earliest visual image of the bay. The Bishop Museum, Honolulu, keeps it safe. The museum's expert and generous librarian, Cynthia Timberlake, has quieted my fears that my images were all wrong with her belief that Ellis made a mirror image of Waimea, for the sake of the engravers. Beaglehole (1967:573, 585, 1222) gives the verbal images of the *Resolution's* crew. There are archeological reviews of Waimea (MacAllister 1933:144-145) and old topographical descriptions (Thrum 1906:115) and environmental impact studies (Bishop Corporation 1974). Kamakau (1961) gives more perspective to our view of Waimea than any other. The prophecy of the priest

Kaopulupulu "The Land is the Sea's" can be found in Kamakau (1961:140).

There is not much of Vancouver that I know that I have not learned from his biographers (Anderson 1960; Godwin 1930) and his most recent editor, Kaye Lamb (Vancouver 1984). The puzzle of the where-abouts of his papers will surely only underline the contingency of any history. The narratives of his execution of the three Hawaiians come from his own account (Vancouver 1798:3:11ff., 1984:797) and witnesses of it (Manby 1929:52-53; Bloxham 1848:44; Howett 1789; Menzies 1793: March 22) and later histories (Dibble 1909:35; Bingham 1848:44; Jarves 1872:78; Fornander 1869:257, Broughton 1804:42; and Iselin n.d.:69). Beaglehole (1967:587, 565) describes some of Hergest's career before he joined the Daedalus. The rest is to be found in Gooch (1786-92).

History in the Making

In the days before my discovery of Gooch, I drew comfort from the fact that the great collector of New Zealand historical documents had searched for the Daedalus and had not found more than I (McNab 1914:1:158-159,2:251). I have reported other stories of her in the Marquesas already (Dening 1980:24-26). I chased the Daedalus through the Historical Records of NSW (HRNSW 1892), and all the original colo-nial secretary's letters published in Historical Records of Australia (HRA 1914) as well as through the Captain's Letters (1790-92:3281, 2917, 3280, 2628) in the Admiralty Papers. I puzzled how Captain New could have been Captain of the Daedalus as well as Lt. Hergest and Lt. Hanson, especially when Haweis (1793:273-279) had reported that Captain New had told this father of the Pacific missions that "immense fields of the heathen world waits only from the zeal of true christians." I had milked the muster rolls of the Discovery and Chatham to catch their exchanges of crew with the Daedalus. Bank's Papers (1791-98:9:88, 122) had reported what Bank's proteges had written him. Banks was post-master of the Pacific. Even Jeremiah Hergest, Hergest's brother, wrote to him asking for information.

Of course there were the Board of Longitude Papers (1791-92), which I had not read very well, William House's (1957) poetic epistle, and the various letters of Lt. Philip King who commanded the penal colony of Norfolk Island (King 1788-99; 1791-94). Let me make a small monu-ment to the crew of the Daedalus by registering their names. Who else will do it? Richard Hergest (Lieut.), Thomas New (Master), Mr. Neil (First Mate), Mr. Moody (Second Mate), William Gooch (AB), Thomas Dobson (Master's Mate), Thomas Franklin (AB), Peter MacDonald (AB),

William Richards (AB), Thomas New (Boy), Mr. Pitts (Supernumerary and secretary to Gooch). Then there was Jack Brask, Jack Jones, Jolly, Baker, Thomas, Bob, Rogger, Mongos, Randall, Gillinghaus, Fisher, Rusden, Cook, Hall, Riley, Moor, Peter (Haggerstein?), Casper, Wright. That makes thirty, the reported complement. Hergest had put the admirals out a little by insisting on at least that number for fear of the natives of the Pacific. A Boy deserted at Deal and three more deserted at Rio. They were replaced by Manuel and two other Portuguese. The lists of the sorry stores that Davison supplied are in Victualling Board (1790-92, 1791). There, my duties are done.

Gooch (1786-92), Ms MM6:48, had many more riches to be plumbed than I have here, but selection and reconstruction are the essence of history's anthropology. There is an infinite number of pasts still to be resurrected out of them. Already Wordsworth's (1877) classic account of *Scholae Acadamicae* at Cambridge and Ball (1889), a history of mathematics at Cambridge, had quoted extensively from Gooch's letters from Caius.

The Brockdish Parish Records, privately owned till a few years ago, are now held in the Norwich Records Office. Traffic now thunders through Brockdish on its way to and from Yarmouth. I did not discover any relics of young William Gooch there, other than the graves of his parents and his sister. My knowledge of Brockdish comes from the great topographer of Norfolk, Francis Blomefield (1805). He held a living at Brockdish but his topography ended twenty or thirty years before Gooch's days. Maybe I should have commented on the sort of history such antiquarians made. It shows how extensive an industry history-making is and how tied the past that we know is to its systems of preservation.

Old William Gooch's will is held in the Norfolk Consistory Court (Will Registers 1818) and the warm memory of him by his pastor, the Rev. Reeves is in the *Christian Remembrancer* (1:1819:19-20). Reading his will I became intrigued with how difficult it is to describe time in both culture and history. While actual living might be "one damn thing after another," the before, now and after of it are all joined. In culture we experience the connections and disconnections. In history we describe them. It is no breach of scientific method to claim to see the time before in the time after.

History Made

Being from the other Cambridge, I was a stranger among very knowing natives when I tried to understand and describe the *mentalité* of Cambridge University and its colleges at the end of the 18th century. I read Christopher Wordsworth's *Scholae Academicae* (1877) several times and "fagged," to use Gooch's term, my way through the classic histories of Cambridge (Winstanley 1922, 1935; Wordsworth 1874; Fuller 1840; Mullinger 1883). I discovered that Henry Gunning (1854), in his reminiscences, had a lien on myth and lore of the times and was the declared master of all the right ways things were done. There was a self-deprecating air about the histories and memoirs of the time as if the years were of no great glory. I read, as far as I could, all that was published at Cambridge and about Cambridge in the years 1785-91. I immersed myself in what remnants there were of those non-glorious years at Caius, such as the Betting Book (1788-99), (in which the fellows, notably among them Brinkley, set their bets in the common room–on the width of the table, on the debts of the Prince of Wales, etc.), the Caius *Gesta* (1787-91), and the relics of various Acts. The signs of ordinary living are mostly leached from these relics of the past. I set myself the task of reading all of Gooch's texts and all the books he had on his shelves. By that, of course, I only rediscovered how full of lateral pursuits any historical inquiry is, and how bending the historian is of these relics to other purposes. The Venns, father and son, were monumental in recording the "historical facts" of Cambridge and Caius. The publications of J. A. Venn (1953), and John Venn (1898, 1901, 1913) were archives in themselves, as was the most recent sensitive history of Caius by Christopher Brooke (1985). Inevitably I was drawn to the same relics of the past as the Venns and Brooke in that small part of their history of Caius that concerned me, but both Venns' and Brooke's histories were saturated with experiences that I had never had. Their joining to their own past enlarged it for me. Robert Willis (1886) made an archeology almost stone by stone of the buildings of Cambridge. I followed him through Caius. I had the need to sense where Gooch had sat and moved. It was only late that I discovered Ben Schneider's *Wordsworth's Cambridge Education* (1957). Schneider is owed a compliment thirty years on for his display of the *mentalité* of Cambridge. He had a masterly touch that any historian would envy, and, if I had no other purposes, I would be embarrassed to put my clumsy images beside his microscopic studies.

I first met Nevil Maskelyne in his patient and careful letters to old William Gooch. His watchfulness for every penny that was owed the father out of the inheritance of his son, I came to know, was matched by his sense of the public nature of his science. I have a half sense that he was not very pleased with the work that William Gooch did in his months as "Astronomer on board the *Daedalus*." Indeed, I have what might be thought to be a disloyal sense that young William was not very good at the practicals of astronomy. He still had too much of the taste of Cambridge's good life for the grind of navigation. While entry into late 18th century astronomy is an ethnographic art–there is no other way of discovering the actual paradigms than in their expression in such relics of them as in the Board of Longitude Papers (1765-1828, 1791, 1791-92)–I confess that I am all at sea on such issues as lunar distances and conic sections. Eric Forbes (1970-71, 1965, 1966-67, 1966, 1974, 1975) made my way easier and he led me to the classic studies such as Gould (1978, 1923); King (1955); Mercer (1972); Taylor (1968). My heart runs cold at the thought of my ignorance and my inability to read the forms and meanings of scientific implements with the perception of such "antiquarians" as Court and Von Rohr (1928-29).

REFERENCES

Admiralty Papers
   1791a *Admiralty Papers*, January-February, 1791. Greenwich: National Maritime Museum. ADM/A/2836.
   1791b *Admiralty Papers*, March-April, 1791. Greenwich: National Maritime Museum. ADM/A/2837.

Anderson, Bern
   1960 *Surveyor of the Sea*. Seattle: University of Washington Press.

Angus, Donald
   1936 "Murder in Hawaii 1792," *Paradise in the Pacific* 48: September 19, 30.

Annual Register
   1807 *Annual Register (1807) of a View of the History, Politics and Literature for the Year*. London: Longman.

Anon.
   1786 *The Norfolk Tour or Travellers' Pocket Companion*. Norwich: R. Beatniffe. 4th ed.
   1788 *Remarks on the Enormous Expense in the Education of Young Men on the University of Cambridge*. London: C. Stalke.
   1898 "Five Hundred and Fiftieth Anniversary." *Caian* 8:136.
   1907 "Heraldry of the College." *Caian* 18:90-106, 181-193.
   1969 *Index of Wills Proved in the Consistory Court of Norwich 1751-1818*. Norwich: Norwich Record Society.

Ball, W.W. Rouse
   1889 *A History of the Study of Mathematics at Cambridge*. Cambridge: Cambridge University Press.

Banks Papers
   1791-1798 "Vancouver's Voyage 1791-98." Sydney: Mitchell Library. Brabourne Collection Vol. 9, A79-2.

Beaglehole, J.C. (ed.)
   1967 *The Journals of Captain James Cook on his Voyages of Discovery III. The Voyage of the Resolution and Discovery 1776-80*. Cambridge: Cambridge University Press. 2 vols.

Bell, Edward
1929-1930 "Log of the Chatham." *Honolulu Mercury* 1: September: 7-26, October: 55-69, November: 79-96, December: 80-91, January: 119-125.

Berkenhout, Dr.
1790 *A Volume of Letters from Dr. Berkenhout to His Son at the University.* Cambridge: Cambridge University Press.

Betting Book
1789-1799 "Betting Book of Fellows, 1789-1799." Cambridge: Caius College Library, MS 655.

Beverley, John
1787 *An Account of the Different Ceremonies Observed in the Senate House of the University of Cambridge Throughout the Year.* Cambridge: Cambridge University Press.

Bingham, Hiram
1848 *A Residence of Twenty-One Years in the Sandwich Islands.* Hartford: Hezekial Huntington.

Bishop Corporation
1974 "An Assessment of Environmental Impact Resulting from Proposed Expansion of Waimea Falls Park. Nov. 1974." Honolulu: Hamilton Library, University of Hawaii Pacific Collection.

Blomefield, Francis
1805 *An Essay Towards a Topographical History of the County of Norfolk,* London: William Miller. Vols. I-V.

Bloxham, Andrew
1925 *Diary of Andrew Bloxham, Naturalist on the Blonde.* Honolulu: B.P. Bishop Museum Special Publications 10.

Broughton, William Robert
1804 *A Voyage of Discovery to the North Pacific Ocean in Her Majesty's Sloop Providence and her Tender in the Years 1795, 1796, 1797, 1798.* London: De Capo Press [1967]. New York.

Board of Longitude Papers
1765-1828 "Meetings of the Board. Royal Minutes 1768-1828." Vol. 3. "Meetings of the Board. Fair Minutes 1765-1828." Vol. 4. "Confirmed Minutes. 1737-1779." Vol. 5. "Confirmed Minutes.

1780-1801." Vol. 6. *Board of Longitude Papers*. Greenwich: National Maritime Museum. Microfilm MRF/L/3.

1791 "List of Instruments." *Board of Longitude Papers*. Vol. 12. Greenwich: National Maritime Museum. Microfilm MRF/L/5.

1791-1792 "Voyage of the Daedalus 1791-2." *Board of Longitude Papers*. Vol. 49. Greenwich: National Maritime Museum. Microfilm MRF/L/25.

1796. "Voyages of Various Ships." *Board of Longitude Papers*. Vol. 58. Greenwich: National Maritime Museum. Microfilm MRF/L/27.

Brockdish Parish Records

1767-1774 "Parish Register of Brockdish in the County of Norfolk." Norwich Records Office, PD 477/2.

1772-1799 "Overseers Records." Norwich: Norwich Records Office, PD 477/43.

1776 "Brockdish Parish Doctor's Bills." Norwich: Norwich Records Office, PD 477/38.

1793 "Churchwarden Accounts." Norwich: Norwich Records Office, PD 477/39.

1813-1894 "Register of Burials in the Parish of Brockdish." Norwich: Norwich Records Office, PD 477/6.

Brooke, Christopher

1985 *A History of Gonville and Caius College*. Suffolk: Boydell Press.

Byron, George

1826 *Voyage of HMS Blonde to the Sandwich Islands, in the Years 1824-1825*. London: Murray.

Burke's

1949 *Burke's Genealogical and Heraldic History of the Peerage*. London: 99th ed. Vol. II.

Buchan, William

1784 *Domestic Medicine or a Treatise on the Prevention and Cure of Disease*. London: W. Strahan.

Caius, John

1904 *The Annals of Gonville and Caius College*. John Venn, ed. Cambridge: Cambridge Antiquarian Society.

Caius Absences Books

1787-1792 "Absences Books and Fines Book. 1787-1792." Cambridge: Gonville and Caius College Archives.

Caius Bursar's Book
1775-1791 "Bursar's Book 1775-1791." Cambridge: Gonville and
Caius College Archives.

Caius Gesta
1787-1792 *"Gesta* 1787-1792." Cambridge: Gonville and Caius
College Archives.

Cambridge
1790 *A Concise and Accurate Description of the University, Town and
County of Cambridge.* Cambridge: Archdeacon. New ed.

Candler, Charles
1896 *Notes on the Parish of Redenhall with Harleston.* London: Harrold
and Sons.

Captains' Letters
1790-1792 "Captains' Letters," *Admiralty Papers.* Sydney: Mitchell
Library. AJCP 3280-3281.

Channer, G.
1909 "The Thesis in the Disputations of the Senior Sophs at
Cambridge 1770-86," IN *Fasciculus Joanni Willis Clark Dicatus.*
Cambridge: Cambridge University Press.

Clark, John Willis
1902 *A Concise Guide to the Town and University of Cambridge.*
Cambridge: Macmillan and Brown.
1908 *Cambridge.* Philadelphia: Lippincolt.

Clegg, M.E.
1957 "Some Eighteenth Century Schools in Suffolk." *Suffolk Review*
1:55-60.

Coleman, Nora E.
1982 *People Poverty and Protest in the Hoxne Hundred 1780-1880.*
Suffolk: Privately Printed.

Colledge, J.J.
1969 *Ships of the Royal Navy: An Historical Index.* Newton Abbot:
David and Charles. 2 vols.

Court, Thomas H. and Moritz, Von Rohr
    1928-1929 "A History of the Development of the Telescope from
        about 1675-1830 or Documents in the Court Collection."
        Transactions of the Optical Society 30:207-260.
    1928-1929 "On the Development of Spectacles in London from the
        End of the 17th Century." *Transactions of the Optical Society* 30:1-21.
    1929-1930 "Contributions to the History of the Worshipful
        Company of Spectacle Makers." *Transactions of the Optical Society*
        31:4-90.

Davison, Alexander
    1750 "Davison, Alexander 1750-1829." *Dictionary of National
        Biography* 14:174-175, London.
    1792 "State of Provisions in N.S.W." Sydney: Mitchell Library MS.,
        AD 97/1.

Dibble, Sheldon
    1909 *A History of the Sandwich Islands.* Honolulu: Thos. G. Thrum.

Dyer, George
    1874 *A History of the University and Colleges of Cambridge.* London:
        Longmans. 2 vols.

Elliot, John
    1791 *A Medical Pocket Book containing a short but plain account of the
        symptoms, causes and methods of cure, of the diseases incident to the
        human body including such as require surgical treatment together with
        the virtues and doses of medicinal compositions and simples extracted
        from the best authors and digested in alphabetical order.* London: n.p.
        3rd ed.

Evans, Edward
    n.d. *Catalogue of a Collection of Engraved Portraits.* Lincoln-in-Fields:
        Privately printed.
    1878 *Excursions in the County of Norfolk.* London: Longman. 2 vols.

Forbes, Eric G.
    1965 "The Foundation and Early Development of the Nautical
        Almanac." *Journal of the Institute of Navigation* 18:391-401.
    1966 "Tobias Mayer's Lunar Tables." *Annals of Science* 22: 105-116.
    1966 "The Origin and Development of the Marine Chronometer."
        Annals of Science 22: 1-25.
    1966-1967 "The Bicentenary of the Nautical Almanac." *British
        Journal for the History of Science.* 3:393-394.

1970-1971 "Index of the Board of Longitude Papers at the Royal Greenwich Observatory." *Journal for the History of Astronomy* 1:167-180, 2:58-70, 132-145.
1974 "The Maskelyne Manuscripts at The Royal Greenwich Observatory." *Journal for the History of Astronomy* 5:67-69.
1975 *Greenwich Observatory.* London: Taylor and Francis.

Fornander, Abraham
1969 *An Account of the Polynesian Race.* Rutland, Vermont: Charles E. Tuttle. 3 vols.

Fuller, Thomas
1840 *The History of the University of Cambridge.* London: Thomas Tegg.

Garland, Martha McMackin
1980 *Cambridge Before Darwin.* Cambridge: Cambridge University Press.

Godwin, George
1930 *Vancouver: A Life, 1757-1798.* London: Phillip Allen.

Gooch, William
1791 "Astronomical Observations and Calculations on The Voyage of the Daedalus. Mr. Gooch's Journal. Journal kept on Board the Daedalus Hir'd Store Ship on a Passage from Rio de Janeiro to the Falkland Islands." *Records of the Board of Longitude.* Vol. 49. Greenwich: National Maritime Museum, Microfilm MRF/L/25.
1786-1792 "Letters, Memoranda and Journal containing the History of Mr. Wm. Gooch, astronomer of the Daedalus Transport from the time of his Entering College in 1786 to his Premature end in 1792 when he was Murdered by the Savages of Woahoo." Cambridge: Cambridge University library, MS Mm 6:48.

Gould, Rupert T.
1923 *The Marine Chronometer.* London: J.P. Potter.
1978 *John Harrison and His Time Keepers.* Greenwich: National Maritime Museum. [*Mariner's Mirror* XXI 1935].

Gray, Arthur
1926 *Cambridge University. An Episodical History.* Cambridge: Heffer.

Gunning, Henry
    n.d. *Customs and Ceremonies of the University of Cambridge*. Cambridge: Cambridge University Press.
    1864 *Reminiscences of the University, Town and County of Cambridge*. London: George Bell. 2 vols.

Guthrie, William,
    1790 *A New Geographical, Historical and Commercial Grammar*. London: G.S. and J. Robinson. 12th ed.

H.M. Nautical Almanac Office.
    1960 "A Modern View of Lunar Distances." *Journal of the Institute of Navigation* 19:131-153.

HRA.
    1914 *Historical Records of Australia*. Sydney: Government Printer.

HRNSW.
    1892 *Historical Records of New South Wales*. Sydney: Government Printer.

Hamilton, Harlan W.
    1969 *Doctor Syntax; A Silhouette of William Corbe, Esq. 1742-1823*. London: Chatto and Windson.

Haselden, Thomas
    1777 *The Seaman's Daily Assistant*. London: J. Mount and T. Page.

Haweis, Thomas
    1793 "Report of a Conference with Captain New of the Daedalus." in *Collection of 38 Draft Letters*. Sydney: Mitchell Library, A1963.

Hewett, George Goodman
    1789 "Marginal Notes to Vancouver's Voyage." Honolulu: University of Hawaii: Hamilton library, Pacific Collection.

Howse, Derek
    1975 *Greenwich Observatory*. London: Taylor and Francis, Vol. 3.

Howse, Derek and Hutchinson, Beresford
    1969 *The Clocks and Watches of Captain James Cook 1769-1969*. London: Antiquarian Horology.

House, William
1957 *A letter from the South Seas by a Voyager on the 'Daedalus', 1792.*
John Earnshaw, ed. Cremorne, N.S.W.: Takarra Press.

Ingraham, Joseph
1971 *Journal of the Brigantine Hope on a Voyage to the North West Coast of North America 1790-92.* Mark D. Kaplanoff, ed. Barre, Massachusetts: Imprint Society.

Iselin, Isaac
n.d. *Journal of a Trading Voyage Around the World 1805-1808.* New York: McIlroy and Emmet.

Jarves, James Jackson
1872 *History of the Hawaiian Islands.* Honolulu: H.M. Whitney.

Johnson, R. Brimley
1928 *The Undergraduate.* London: Stanley Paul.

Ka Mooolelo Hawaii
1984 *Ka Mooolelo Hawaii.* Dorothy M. Kahananui, ed. Honolulu: University Press of Hawaii.

Kamakau, Samuel
n.d. "Moolelo o Hawaii." Honolulu: Bishop Museum Library.
1961 *Ruling Chiefs of Hawaii.* Honolulu: Kamehameha Schools Press.
1964 *Ka Po'e Kahiko. The People of Old.* Mary Kawena Pukui, trans. Honolulu: Bishop Museum Press.
1976 *The Works of the People of Old. Na Hau a ka Po'e Kahiko.* Honolulu: Bishop Museum Press.

Keill, John
1778 *An Introduction to the True Astronomy.* London: J.F. and C. Rivington. 126th ed.

King, Henry C.
1955 *The History of the Telescope.* London: Charles Griffin.
1788-1789 "Letter-Book, Norfolk Island." Sydney: Mitchell Library, MS C187.
1791-1794 "Journal of Transactions, Norfolk Island." Sydney: Mitchell Library, MS A1687.

Knight, Frida
1971 *University Rebel. The Life of William Frend 1757-1841.* London: Victor Gollancz.

Knight, R.J.B. (ed.)
1977 *Guide to the Manuscripts in the National Maritime Museum.* London: Mansell. 2 vols.

Kuykendall, Ralph S.
1938 *The Hawaiian Kingdom.* Honolulu: University Press of Hawaii. 3 vols.

Le Sage, Alain Reve
1789 *Le Diable Boiteux avec les entretiens serieux et comiques des cheminées de Madrid et les bequilles du dit diable par M.B. de S.* Paris: Abbe Bordelon.

Little Goody Two-Shoes
1766 *The History of Little Goody Two-Shoes; otherwise called Mrs Margery Two-Shoes with the means she acquired her learning and wisdom and its consequence there of to her estate; set forth at large for the benefit of those who from a state of rags and care and having shoes but half a pair their fortune and their fame would fix and gallop in a coach and six. See the original manuscript in the Vatican at Rome and cuts by Michael Angelo. Illustrated with the comments of our great modern critics.* London: J. Newberry. 3rd ed. Facsimile Reproduction 1881, Griffith and Farran.

Lloyds
1790-1796 *Lloyds Register of British and Foreign Shipping.* London: Lloyds.

McAllister, J. Gilbert
1933 *Archaeology of Oahu.* Honolulu: B.P. Bishop Museum Bulletin 104.

McKay, Andrew
1793 *The Theory and Practice of Finding Longitude at sea or land to which are added various methods of determining the latitude of a place and variance of the compass with new tables.* London: J. Sewell. 2 vols.

McNab, Robert
1914 *Historical Records of New Zealand.* Wellington: Government Printer. 2 vols.

Mainwaring, G. E.
1930 *A Bibliography of British Naval History.* London: George Routledge.

Manby, Thomas.
1929 "Journal of Vancouver's Voyage to the Pacific Ocean (1791-93)." *Honolulu Mercury* 1: June 11-25, July 23-45, August, 39-55.

Marshall, James Stirrat and Carrie
1955 *Adventure in Two Hemispheres.* Vancouver.

Mathias, P. and A. W. H. Pearsall (eds.)
1971 *Shipping: A Survey of Historical Records.* Newton Abbot: David and Charles.

May, W. E.
1945 "Early Reflecting Instruments." *Nautical Magazine* 153:21-26.

Meany, Edmond S.
1907 *Vancouver's Discovery of Puget Sound.* New York: Macmillan.

Menzies, Archibald
1790-1794 "Journal of Vancouver's Voyage 1790-1794." Sydney: Mitchell Library. ADD MS 32641. Microfilm FM 4/16.
1923 *Journal of Vancouver's Voyage April to October 1792.* C. F. Newcombe, ed. Victoria B.C: W. H. Cullin.

Mercer, Vaudrey
1972 *John Arnold and Son. Chronometer Makers 1762-1843.* London: Antiquarian Horological Society.

Millburn, John R.
1976 *Benjamin Martin. Author, Instrument-Maker and 'Country Showman'.* Leyden: Noordkoff.

Minson, William Harvey
1957 "The Hawaiian Journal of Manuel Quimper." Honolulu: Master of Arts Thesis. University of Hawaii.

Moore, John Hamilton
1791 *The Practical Navigator and Seaman's New Daily Assistant. Being an Epitome of Navigation.* London: B. Law and Son. 9th ed.

Mullinger, J. B.
    1883 *The University of Cambridge.* Cambridge: Cambridge University Press. 3 vols.

Namier, Sir Lewis and Brooke, John
    1964 *The House of Commons 1754-1790.* London: History of Parliament Trust HMSO.

Nelson, Robert
    1749 *The Practice of True Devotion, in relation to the End, as well as the Means of Religion, with an Office for Holy Communion.* London: B. Dod. 12th ed.

Nicolas, Sir Nicolas Harris
    1844 *The Despatches and Letters of Vice Admiral Lord Viscount Nelson.* London: H. Colbourn.

Papa Ii, John
    1959 *Fragments of Hawaiian History.* Honolulu: B.P. Bishop Museum.

Parliamentary Papers
    1806-1807 "The Third Report of the Commissioners of Military Enquiry." *Parliamentary Papers: Reports and Other Matters 1806-7:ii.*

Poll for Election
    1790 *The Poll for the Election of Two Representatives in Parliament for the University of Cambridge on Thursday June 17, 1790.* Cambridge: Cambridge University Press.

Purkis, William
    1789 *The Evils which may arise to the Constitution of Great Britain from the Influence of a too powerful nobility.* London:n.p.

Register
    1758-1795 "Register of Books Taken Out 1758-1795." Cambridge: Caius College Library MS. 3 vols.

Roberts, Julian
    1965 "The 1765 Edition of Goody Two-Shoes." *British Museum Quarterly* 29:67-70.

Robertson, John
    1780 *The Elements of Navigation.* London: T. Nourse. 2 vols.

Rye, Walter
1887 *An Index to Norfolk Topography.* London: Longman.

Sadler, D.H.
1968 "The Bicentenary of the Nautical Almanac." *Journal of the Institute of Navigation 21:6-18.*

Sahlins, Marshall
1981 *Historical Metaphors and Mythical Realities: Structure in the Early History of the Sandwich Islands.* Association For Social Anthropology in Oceania, Special Publications No. 1. Ann Arbor: University of Michigan Press.
1985 *Islands of History.* Chicago: University of Chicago Press.

Schneider, Ben Ross
1957 *Wordsworth's Cambridge Education.* Cambridge: Cambridge University Press.

Schools Arguments
1784 "Schools Arguments." Cambridge: Caius College Library MS 689/776.

Scott, Sir Robert Forsythe
1931 *Admissions to the College of St. John the Evangelist in the University of Cambridge.* Cambridge: Cambridge University Press.

Smith, J.
1774 "College History: Miscellaneous." Cambridge: Caius College Library MS.

Stevens, Thomas
1790 *Serious Cautions to Young Students. A Sermon Preached before the University of Cambridge on Commencement Sunday, July 4, 1790.* Cambridge: n.p.

Stone, William Macey
1939 "The History of Little Goody Two-Shoes." *American Antiquarian Society Proceedings* 49:333-370.

Tanner, J.R. (ed.)
1917 *The Historical Register of the University of Cambridge.* Cambridge: Cambridge University Press.

Taylor, E.G.R.
1968 "Navigation in the Days of Captain Cook." *Journal of the Institute of Navigation* 21:256-276.

Thrum, Thos. G.
1906 "A Visit to Waimea, Oahu, Scene of the Daedalus Tragedy of May, 1792." *Hawaiian Almanac and Annual for 1906:* 113-117.
1917 "Brief Sketch of the Life and Labours of S.M. Kamakau, Hawaiian Historian." *Hawaiian Historical Society Annual Report* 1917:26:40-61.

Valeri, Valerio
1985 *Kingship and Sacrifice. Ritual and Society in Ancient Hawaii.* Chicago: University of Chicago Press.

Vancouver, George
1798 *A Voyage of Discovery to the North Pacific Ocean and Round the World.* London: G.G. and J. Robinson. 3 vols.
1984 *A Voyage of Discovery to the North Pacific Ocean and Round the World. 1791-1795.* W. Kaye Lamb, ed. London: Hakluyt Society. 4 vols.

Venn, John
1898 *Biographical History of Gonville and Caius College 1349-1897.* Cambridge: Cambridge University Press. Vol. 11, 1713-1897.
1901 *Caius College.* London: F.E. Robinson.
1913 *Early Collegiate Life.* Cambridge: W. Heffer.

Venn, J.A.
1953 *Alumni Cantabrigiensis.* Cambridge: Cambridge University Press.

Victoria History.
1906 *Victoria History of the County of Norfolk.* London: A. Constable.
1965 *Victoria History of the County of Warwick.* London: Dawsons.
1975 *Victoria History of the County of Suffolk.* London: Dawsons.

Victualling Board
1790-1792 *Admiralty Papers.* Greenwich: National Maritime Museum. ADM/D/37.
1791 "Victualling Board to Admiralty." *Admiralty Papers.* Greenwich: National Maritime Museum. ADM/D/37.

Vince, S.
  1790 *A Treatise on Practical Astronomy.* Cambridge: Cambridge
  University Press.
  1797 *The Heads of a Course of Lectures on Experimental Philosophy.*
  Cambridge: Cambridge University Press.
  1801 *Elements of Astronomy Designed for the Use of Students in the
  University.* Cambridge: Cambridge University Press. 2nd ed.

Walder, David
  1978 *Nelson.* London: Hamilton.

Watson, Richard
  1787 *An Address to Young Persons after Confirmation.* Cambridge:
  Cambridge University Press.

White, William,
  1836 *History, Gazeteer and Directory of Norfolk.* Sheffield: R. Leader.

Will Registers
  1818 "Will Registers. Norfolk Consistory Court." Norwich: Norwich
  Records Office. MF101, 1818, 1819, FF1-224.

Willis, Robert
  1886 *The Architectural History of the University of Cambridge.*
  Cambridge: Cambridge University Press. 3 vols.

Winstanley, D.A.
  1922 *The University of Cambridge in the 18th Century.* Cambridge:
  Cambridge University Press.
  1935 *Unreformed Cambridge.* Cambridge: Cambridge University Press.

Wordsworth, Christopher
  1874 *Social Life at the English Universities in the 18th Century.*
  Cambridge: Deighton Bell.
  1877 *Scholae Academicae: Some Account of the Studies at the English
  Universities in the Eighteenth Century.* Cambridge: Cambridge
  University Press.

Wright, Thomas
  1847 *Memorials of Cambridge.* London: D. Bogue. 2 vols.